D0475307

The Great Romances of the Bible

Love Stories God Told

DAVID & HEATHER KOPP

HARVEST HOUSE PUBLISHERS
EUGENE, OREGON 97402

Dedication

For: BRAD&KIM HAYES

Copyright © 1998 by David and Heather Kopp
Published by Harvest House Publishers
Eugene, Oregon 97402

Library of Congress Cataloging-in-Publication Data
Kopp, David, 1949-
    Love stories God told / David and Heather Kopp.
       p.   cm.
    ISBN 1-56507-823-3
    1. Married people in the Bible. 2. Marriage—Religious aspects—
Christianity. 3. Love—Religious aspects—Christianity. 4. Bible stories, English.
I. Kopp, Heather Harpham. 1964–   . II. Title
    BS579. H8K66   1998
    261. 8′3581—dc21   97-34260
                                                   CIP

Design and Production by Koechel Peterson & Associates, Minneapolis, Minnesota

Illustration, page 18-19: *Temperantia*, 1872 by Sir Edward Burne-Jones (1833-98).
Christie's Images/Bridgeman Art Library, London/New York

Scripture quotations are from the Holy Bible, New International Version®. Copyright © 1973,
1978, 1984 by the International Bible Society. Used by permission of Zondervan Publishing House.
The "NIV" and "New International Version" trademarks are registered in the United States Patent
and Trademark Office by International Bible Society.

Printed in the United States of America.

98 99 00 01 02 03 04 05 06 07/IP/10 9 8 7 6 5 4 3 2 1

Presented to:

_____

On the occasion of:

_____

Date:

_____

With love from:

_____

Whoever

lives in love

lives in God,

and God

1 JOHN 4:16

in them.

The Story Behind the Love Stories

Has not the Lord

made them one?

In flesh and spirit

MALACHI 2:15

they are His.

THIS BOOK BEGAN UNDER A PINE TREE one spring afternoon with a simple question. We were enjoying a blanket for two and the warm sun on our faces when one of us asked, "Do you think God really cares about romance?"

Everyone knows God is love. And he wants us to love each other. But that's the serious, sacrificial, Sunday kind of love. What about love at first sight? Love that's a thumping in the heart and a longing in the night?

As we looked to the Bible for the answer, we were delighted to discover an abundance of couples in love. In fact, God took time to record details of first looks, tender conversations, and physical attractions. In some of the stories, he got directly involved playing matchmaker. And he devoted an entire book of the Bible, the Song of Songs, to expound on the mysteries of passion and pursuit.

Our purpose in retelling God's love stories (versus using the text of Scripture) was to help you meet the flesh-and-blood people behind the familiar Bible characters—women and men with whom we can immediately identify. Like us, some of them rose to great acts of devotion, ardor, and sacrifice under the influence of love. And like us, others made small or foolish choices and suffered painful losses.

Regardless of each couple's success, we're thankful that God took time to include their stories. After meeting these lovers, we're sure you'll be inspired to cherish your own love relationships with more understanding and commitment. And we hope you'll make the same wonderful discovery we did: As God pulls on the thread of each human love story, he is really weaving together the greatest love story of all—his eternal love for and pursuit of each one of us.

David and Heather Kopp

TABLE *of* CONTENTS

ADAM&EVE
Love Is a New Beginning

Awake, north wind,

and come, south wind!

Blow on my garden,

that its fragrance

may spread abroad.

Let my lover come into his garden

and taste its choice fruits.

Song of Songs 4:16

"Come into
my garden...
Taste the
choice fruits
of love."

ADAM&EVE

The Marriage:

God made Eve from Adam's rib
and "he brought her to the man."
No ceremony mentioned.

Children:

Cain, Abel, and Seth named;
many others assumed.

Most Memorable Scene:

Adam awakens to see Eve,
the first woman,
made from his own body.

Greatest Obstacle:

Sustaining their love after they
were banished from Eden.

Compatibility:

Very high; the only two people
created by God to exactly complete
and compliment each other.

Adam, what have we done? Adam, what have we done? Adam, what have we done?

Is God still

8

ABOUT HIM

Name:
Adam, "of the ground."

Age:
Probably corresponded physically
to an 18- to 25-year-old.

Appearance:
The ultimate man,
reflecting the beautiful possibilities
of all the races to come.

Personality:
Unknown, but he was the
prototype for all humans.

Family Background:
No father or mother besides God,
his Maker.

Place in History:
First man; famous for causing sin
to enter the world by eating
the forbidden fruit offered by Eve.

ABOUT HER

Name:
Eve, "the life-giving one."

Age:
Probably corresponded physically
to a 16- to 22-year-old.

Appearance:
Traditionally considered the most
beautiful woman who ever lived.

Personality:
Like Adam, unknown.

Family Background:
No parents; made from Adam's rib;
"born" into a marriage.

Place in History:
Last being God created; famous
for succumbing to the serpent
and eating of the forbidden
fruit in Eden.

love to us?

Love Is a New Beginning

GENESIS 2,3

For this reason

a man will leave

his father and

mother and be

united to his wife

and they will

GENESIS 2:24

become one flesh.

AS THE MORNING SUN ROSE IN A BLUE SKY, Eve's bare toes touched the dew-covered grass. She stepped gracefully through a soft green landscape with her lover and husband, Adam. He radiated strength and laughter. Together they were a perfect miracle, she thought. And this new day of spice breezes and peace belonged to them completely. . . .

"Ah, Eden . . . home . . . !" she sighed.

Later, the couple made a bed in the shade of their favorite spreading kumquat tree. Every morning, lying under this green tent or trailing their feet in a stream, the man and woman talked. In the afternoon, they swirled around each other like butterflies in a dance of passion, and then napped like two children, arms flung wide. . . .

Here in Eden, love was so close to the surface of living that Adam and Eve hardly noticed it. *Love . . .* breathe in. *Be loved . . .* breathe out. Whenever the lovers tried to name it, only one word came to their lips—*God.* His name was Love, and Adam and Eve were his Beloved. Swept up in his presence, they knew nothing at all but love.

Until the day they wanted to know more. . . .

NOW THEY COWERED IN THE BUSHES. Actually, they kept to separate bushes—Adam under a tangle of grapevines, and Eve behind a thick tamarisk. They fumbled with a lapful of fig leaves and reeds, trying to piece together body coverings.

Only hours ago, something like a curtain had fallen away from their eyes and they'd been startled to discover they were naked. Suddenly they wanted to hide, to conceal their bodies—perfect as they were—even from themselves.

When the curtain fell, everything else in the Garden of Love seemed strangely unfamiliar, apart, even dangerous.

What troubled Adam most was the awareness that the inner workings of his heart had altered fearfully. A hubbub of dark thoughts and unwanted cravings now haunted him. Was his wife experiencing the same terrors?

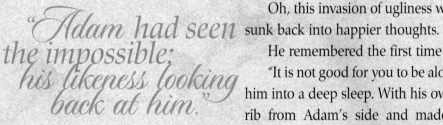

"E- Eve. . . ." His voice quavered across the patch of grass between them. "Eve, are we dying? Is this death?" Hadn't God said they would die? Adam had never seen anything die.

"How should I know?" Eve mumbled into her lap.

Adam studied Eve. *How much she has changed since this morning.* Her whole being had collected shadows. Her eyes had faded to only one color; her hair, once a shining invitation, now hung down in a thick barrier. Or was it only the sourness in himself that made him see her differently, made him feel suddenly suspicious about her every word and gesture?

Oh, this invasion of ugliness was too much to bear. Adam sunk back into happier thoughts.

He remembered the first time he saw her.

"Adam had seen the impossible; his likeness looking back at him."

"It is not good for you to be alone," God had said, and put him into a deep sleep. With his own hands, God had taken a rib from Adam's side and made a miracle. When Adam opened his eyes, he had seen the impossible: his likeness looking back at him. Only it *wasn't* him. This being was excitingly more and different—yet reassuringly like him. And she was so beautiful.

For the first time, Adam experienced desire. *"This is now bone of my bones and flesh of my flesh; she shall be called 'woman,' for she was taken out of man!"* (Genesis 2:23).

Yes, Eve had been taken from him, created by God from his own body. And then given back to him. From the first look, she had been both a gift and a necessity, a longing that burned like fire and a fulfillment that soothed like water—and left him completely happy.

But that was before "his own body" had betrayed him. . . .

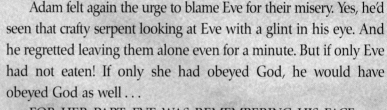

*"Look for your other half
who walks always next to you
and tends to be who you aren't."*

ANTONIO MACHADO

Adam felt again the urge to blame Eve for their misery. Yes, he'd seen that crafty serpent looking at Eve with a glint in his eye. And he regretted leaving them alone even for a minute. But if only Eve had not eaten! If only she had obeyed God, he would have obeyed God as well . . .

FOR HER PART, EVE WAS REMEMBERING HIS FACE—not Adam's, but the serpent's. His hypnotic eyes, smooth pink tongue, and smoother voice. How his cold beauty still coiled around her mind. Yes, she had met the enemy of her happiness face to face— and hadn't even recognized him until too late.

Why had she found his words so disarming, so convincing? "Did God really say . . . ?" the serpent had sighed. "He knows that when you eat of this fruit your eyes will open and you will become like God . . . ."

Of course, the fruit had been tempting—smooth, firm, plump. Worth at least one bite.

Now this—two lovers skulking in the bushes.

Eve pushed tear-soaked hair back from her face. Would her husband ever look at her the same? Yet she couldn't bear his eyes now anyway. She would leave Adam here and go to the stream to try to wash the hurt away. Maybe she would just find a place to crawl away and hide. Maybe . . .

They both look up startled from their private thoughts. They heard what they dreaded, the sound of God approaching.

"This is stupid, trying to hide!" Adam growled to Eve, grabbing his silly arrangement of leaves. "God knows exactly where we are—and what we've done!"

*"EVE! ADAM!
My beloved...
where are you?"*

"But I don't want to go out there. I can't bear to let him see me...." Eve's voice trailed off.

Now they heard God call again. "Eve! Adam! My beloved...where are you?" The Lord of the Garden's voice wafted through the trees like deep music.

But neither of them could answer.

Of course, it was no use to hide. "I'm here, Lord," Adam finally said.

"And why are you hiding?" God asked. His presence surrounded them.

"I heard you coming and I was afraid," Adam said shakily. "I'm naked, so I hid."

"And who told you that you were naked?" God asked. "Have you eaten from the tree I commanded you not to eat from?"

Adam shot an accusing glance toward his wife. "Eve—the woman you made for me—" he blurted, "she gave me fruit from the tree. Otherwise I wouldn't have eaten it!"

For the first time since the disaster with the snake, Eve locked eyes with her husband. She gasped in disbelief. He was blaming it all on her!

God's voice broke in. "Eve, what is this you have done?"

"The snake you made lied to me!" she cried. "He tricked me into eating the fruit!"

After Adam and Eve had stumbled through their excuses, they could only wait, heads hung, for God's response. When he spoke, he told them that what they had done would change everything. Nothing could ever be the same again.

He spoke first to Eve. *"I will greatly increase your pains in child-bearing; with pain you will give birth to children"* (Genesis 3:16).

And then to Adam. *"Cursed is the ground because of you; through painful toil you will eat of it all the days of your life ... By the sweat of your*

Love IN BIBLE TIMES

The Mystery of Male and Female

When God created man, he created him in the likeness of God. He created them male and female. Genesis 5:1,2

Why didn't God make just one of each living thing? Surely, He could have created another means for continuing a species besides male and female genders. Why *two* that are the same, yet opposite—and compelled to come together?

Rabbis of old taught that God created Eve so that Adam would understand that he was not God's equal. Though Adam had been given dominion over the earth, he must remember that God alone has no counterpart in the universe.

Scripture makes it clear that Adam was created *incomplete* without Eve. In a world untouched by sin, where Adam literally "had it all," he still needed woman. God called each of His creative acts, "Good!" But God called it "not good" for Adam to live alone.

Male and female had perfect harmony—until sin brought conflict between them (and the genders) forever.

Fortunately, God also created love. Through love and marriage, we become more than just male and female. We become "one flesh"—the beautiful sum of our differences.

brow you will eat your food until you return to the ground, since from it you were taken; for dust you are and to dust you will return" (Genesis 3:17-19).

Pain. Longing. Toil. Sweat. Becoming dust—death! The words hung like a veil of sadness in the afternoon air.

Then, right in front of their eyes, God showed them what death was. He killed two gazelles and stripped the skins from the carcasses. Adam and Eve watched, horrified. The limp bodies; the glazed, sightless eyes; and the steady dripping of red tears into the dust. So this was death.

When God had formed the animal skins into soft leather garments, he gave them to Adam and Eve. "These are for you to cover yourselves," he said.

And then God led them to the gates of Eden and told them they could never return. They would never again see the place the Lord of Love had made as a gift for his beloved ones. Another kind of life waited for them now…

That night Adam and Eve huddled separately beneath a tree they didn't know, an unfamiliar, unfriendly tree. The cold crowded in. They clutched their new garments tightly. Behind them, the night sky blazed with light from the angel who guarded Eden's gate.

"Would Adam still find himself— and something more— in her face?"

Eve cried out, "Adam, what have we done? Is God still love to us? Will he still walk and talk with us?"

"Perhaps, if we obey what God says now, we will still be his beloved," Adam replied.

"But … what if we cannot help but disobey God again?"

Adam understood her question, but he didn't answer. For the first time ever they lay untouching, unwilling to lie in each other's arms, and yet afraid of this new desire to be apart. All night, they hoped to hear the Lord approaching. But they heard only hungry animals on the prowl.

AS THE MORNING SUN ROSE IN A BLUE SKY, Eve's bare toes touched thorns. She looked down at her body, wrapped in the dead creature's skins, and over at her husband Adam. She peered around at the strange landscape of dry plains and wondered what the day would bring.

Would desire follow them here? Would she and Adam ever dance again? Would more blood be shed? And would Adam still find himself—and something more—in her face?

She gazed down at her still sleeping husband.

How could they make a new beginning? *Love* … breathe in. *Be loved* … breathe out.

"Oh, Adam …," she sighed. Carefully she reached over to slide her arms around her husband. ❧

MEDITATION
for Married Lovers

Beyond the Garden Walls

ADAM AND EVE'S story was the first—and in some ways the last—human experience of perfect love. No marriage would ever again be as simple or beautiful. Whereas in Eden life had been easy, and romance came as naturally as laughter, now the two lovers had to work at everything, including love.

Sound familiar?

To this day, when we discover ourselves tumbling happily into love, we experience a slice of Eden. Everything seems perfect, the birds are always singing, our hearts thrill. Our beloved miraculously completes us. "You are bone of my bone, flesh of my flesh!" we cry.

But as time passes, we eat from the tree of knowledge. Our eyes are opened to our lover's faults and shortcomings. Soon, work and family stresses further test our feelings and our ideals. Gradually, love, as we once knew it, takes a "fall."

But the first love story doesn't end there, and ours needn't either. God did not abandon Adam and Eve, nor they each other. Marriage would never be perfect again, but love would still be possible—and more precious than ever!

And that is the hope that echoes down to us through time. We treasure our glimpses of Eden, but the power of our union reaches far beyond the Garden walls. When the bliss of romance falters, another kind of love promises comfort, forgiveness, healing, and hope. And who could treasure these gifts more than fallen humans?

In the familiar embrace of our beloved, we hear God exclaim again, "It is good!" And we find new strength to face our world together.

"In the familiar embrace of our beloved, we hear God exclaim again, 'It is good!'"

ISAAC&REBEKAH
Love Is a Gift of Angels

How beautiful you are, my darling!

Oh how beautiful!

Your eyes behind your veil are doves.

Your lips are like a scarlet ribbon;

your mouth is lovely.

Your two breasts are like two fawns

like twin fawns of a gazelle

that browse among the lilies.

You have stolen my heart, my sister, my bride.

you have stolen my heart

with one glance of your eyes.

Song of Songs 4:1-9

"You have
stolen my
heart

with one
glance
of your eyes."

ISAAC&REBEKAH

The Marriage:
Arranged by an angel.

Children:
Jacob and Esau, twins.

Most Memorable Scene:
First sight of one another.

Greatest Obstacle:
Trusting that God was making the match.

Compatibility:
Probably good; they shared
a heritage of faith and family.

ABOUT HIM

Name:
Isaac, "laughter."

Age:
40.

Appearance:
Unknown.

Personality:
A loner, peace-loving, trusting,
loved his mother.

Family Background:
Only son of Abraham and Sarah,
born in their old age.

Place in History:
Called "the child of promise";
second in line of Jewish patriarchs.

"Drink,
she said brightly,

ABOUT HER

Name:
Rebekah, "flattery."

Age:
Probably 15 to 18.

Appearance:
Very beautiful.

Personality:
High-spirited, helpful,
but portrayed as scheming
later in life.

Family Background:
Grew up in Mesopotamia;
the grandniece of Abraham.

Place in History:
She and Eve are the only Bible brides
"personally selected" by God.

As he watched
the lovely maiden,
he found himself
hoping she might
be the one
my lord,"
and quickly lowered the jar.

Love Is a Gift of Angels
GENESIS 24

He went out to the field one evening to meditate, and as he looked up, he saw camels approaching. Rebekah also looked up and

saw Isaac.

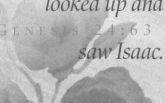

When the old servant heard Abraham's request, his eyes widened with surprise. In all his years of loyal service, his duties had never included matchmaking.

Eliezer knew that ever since Sarah died, Abraham had been fretting about getting a wife for Isaac, his miracle son born to Sarah in her old age. Abraham was worried that with Isaac's mother gone, his son would get lonely and—God forbid!—marry one of the local pagan women.

Now, Abraham was asking Eliezer, his chief servant, to travel all the way to their people in Paddan-Aram in order to bring back a wife for Isaac.

"But what if the woman won't come back with me without meeting Isaac?" he asked doubtfully. "Then can I take your son back there with me?"

"Never!" Abraham exclaimed. "The Lord promised me, 'To your offspring I will give *this* land.'" He spread his bony arms wide. "*This* land!" he repeated. "And now, this same God will send an angel ahead of you to help you get a wife for my son."

Upon hearing this, Eliezer promised to do exactly as his master wished.

Soon he and his men were making the 700-mile journey away from Canaan and toward Paddan-Aram. With each step Eliezer heard the soft clinking of coins, gold ornaments, and inlaid ivory treasures hidden in his bags. The sound reminded him of a young girl's laughter—and that he carried dowry gifts for a new bride for Isaac.

Isaac himself had appeared to have hesitations about the plan, and offered a few suggestions to his father's chief servant. "Let her be beautiful," he'd whispered to Eliezer as he prepared his camel's pack. "Let her be as beautiful and as radiant and good as my mother."

The old servant had nodded and grunted. "I will do my best for my master Abraham," he'd answered sternly. "So far as his son, Isaac, is concerned . . ." His eyes had twinkled mischievously at the young man. "I will do my best for him also."

"Let her be beautiful," he whispered to Eliezer as he prepared his camel's pack.

When finally Eliezer's caravan arrived by a well outside the town of Nahor in the region of Paddan-Aram, Eliezer lifted his hands in prayer. "See, I am standing beside this spring, and the daughters of the townspeople are coming out to draw water," he prayed. "May it be, Lord, that when I say to a girl, 'Please let down your jar that I may have a drink,' and she says, 'Drink, and I'll water your camels too'—let her be the one you have chosen for Isaac."

Before he had even finished praying, a young woman approached carrying a jar on her shoulder. She was a radiant beauty. Eliezer could tell by her dress that she had never been married.

When the girl went down to the well and filled her jar, Eliezer went to her and said, "Please give me a little water."

"Drink, my lord," she said brightly, and quickly lowered the jar to give him a drink. The servant drank slowly. As he watched the lovely maiden, he found himself hoping she might be the one. But would God answer his prayer so quickly?

After the girl had given Eliezer a drink, she said, "I'll draw water for your camels too, until they have finished drinking."

For the next hour, Eliezer watched in amazement and with growing excitement as this energetic young woman brought water to his whole caravan. When the camels had finished drinking, Eliezer approached.

"Whose daughter are you?" he asked. "And please tell me, is there room in your father's house for us to spend the night?"

"I am Rebekah," she offered, "the daughter of Bethuel." Then she added, "We have plenty of straw and fodder, as well as room for you to spend the night."

BY NOW ELIEZER WAS NEARLY LEAPING WITH HAPPINESS. "Praise be to the Lord, God of my master Abraham!" he blurted out to the startled girl. "He has not abandoned his kindness and faithfulness to my master. As for me, the Lord has led me on the journey to the house of my master's relatives."

With a flourish, Eliezer reached in his saddlebags and pulled out carefully wrapped jewelry—including a gold nose ring and two gold bracelets. These he held out to young Rebekah.

She shyly took the gifts, offered a few fumbling words of thanks, and then turned and ran in the direction of home.

When Rebekah's brother, Laban, saw the exquisite jewelry his sister was waving around, he hurried back to the well. "Come, you who are blessed by the Lord," he called to Eliezer and his men. "Why are you standing out here?"

Soon Eliezer was seated around the table with Rebekah's family. But he refused to eat until he had told them the nature of his mission. He explained why Abraham had sent him. Then he recounted in detail how he had kneeled by the well and proposed a deal with God to find the right bride for Isaac. "Before I finished praying in my heart," he said, "Rebekah came out, with her jar on her shoulder!"

Everyone was smiling broadly now, winking at Rebekah.

Eliezer continued, "When I asked for a drink, she offered me her jar of water and said, 'Drink, and I'll draw water for your camels too!'"

"Ahhh . . . !" everyone exclaimed delightedly. "What a touching story! And what a miracle!"

Then Eliezer turned to Laban and Bethuel. "Please, show kindness to my master and tell me if your answer is yes or no."

The men of the household could only raise their palms to heaven. "This is from the Lord," they said as one. "*We can say nothing to you one way or the other. Here is Rebekah; take her and go, and let her become the*

"Around the fire each night Rebekah plied Eliezer with questions about his master's mystery son."

wife of your master's son, as the Lord has directed" (Genesis 24:50,51).

Eliezer rose, and bowed for a moment of thanks to the Lord. Then he brought out more gifts for Rebekah—gold and silver jewelry along with finely embroidered clothing. He also presented her brother and mother with costly gifts.

The next morning, Eliezer announced that he was ready to return home. The family was surprised. "Please, let the girl remain with us ten days or so; then you may go."

But when Eliezer persisted, the family decided to leave the decision up to Rebekah. She said simply, "I will leave now."

And leave she did.

When the time came to depart, Bethuel's family gathered around the bride-to-be and pronounced an ancient blessing on her:

Our sister, may you increase to thousands upon thousands;
may your offspring possess the gates of their enemies (Genesis 24:60).

Then, Rebekah and her maidservants rode away from her family with Eliezer's caravan toward marriage to a man she had never seen. . . .

Day after day on the journey back to Canaan, Rebekah tried to imagine the new life that awaited her. Around the fire each night, she plied Eliezer with questions about his master's mystery son. How did he live? What was his family like? What did he look like?

Eliezer tried to explain, but found himself tongue-tied. "He is a chosen son," he would say, as if this should be enough to satisfy the curiosity of any bride-to-be.

Meanwhile, one evening in Canaan Isaac had gone out to the field to stroll and meditate. As was usually the case lately, he was distracted by anticipation and endless questions. However, this evening, he looked up and saw camels approaching. Soon he could see that it was Eliezer's caravan—and traveling with him, several women.

Love IN BIBLE TIMES

Negotiating for a Wife

The way a man secured a wife in Bible times resembles how we negotiate to buy a house: success depended on sufficient finances, a good agent, and smart negotiating.

First, the suitor's family needed enough resources for a sizable down payment —the *mohar*, or "brideprice." Besides money, this could take the form of work or gifts. The suitor was represented to the family of the bride by an "agent" who knew how much the suitor could afford. When the agent and the suitor's father arrived at the prospective bride's home, they would decline food or drink to indicate the serious nature of the business at hand ("I will not eat," said Isaac's servant, "until I have told you my business").

Both sides negotiated until an agreement was reached. Then everyone exchanged congratulations and celebrated together over a meal.

The brideprice helped compensate her family for the loss of their daughter. But the bride's parents gave her a "dowry"—a personal wedding gift of valuables, property, or servants (Rebekah, for example, took five maids to her new home).

Traditions of brideprice and arranged marriages are still practiced in Eastern cultures. But then as now, the aim is always to find not just a wife for the home, but a bride for the heart.

At that very moment, Rebekah also looked up and saw Isaac. "Eliezer," she asked, "who is that man in the field coming to meet us?" The man in the field was looking right at her.

"He is my master's son, Isaac," Eliezer answered.

A faint smile hovered on Rebekah's lips as she covered her face with her veil.

Then Isaac walked up, and Eliezer dismounted and bowed to the ground. With his face beaming, he began, "Praise be to the Lord, God of my master Abraham, for leading me by an angel on the right road...!"

Riding back to the family tents, Eliezer told Isaac the story of the young girl at the well, exactly as it had happened, from start to finish. In the days that followed, the old servant reminded Isaac at every opportunity, "This is from the Lord!"

Little did he know that Isaac himself had also whispered the same phrase in his new bride's ear.

When the whole clan arrived for the wedding feast, it was apparent to Abraham and to everyone that the angel had made a good match. Even behind her veil, who could mistake the light in Rebekah's eyes? Who could fail to notice that Isaac was far more bright and talkative than usual? What had been rumored must be true, the guests decided. From that first glance in the fields, Isaac had been in love with his young Rebekah.

Eliezer watched the happy proceedings with great relief and glowing pride. Gazing on Rebekah's wholesome, radiant beauty, he felt sure Isaac's mother Sarah would have approved. An angel had brought bride and groom together, and now, perhaps, an angel had come to stay in Isaac's tent. ❧

"If I leave all for thee, wilt thou exchange and be all for me?"

ELIZABETH BARRETT BROWNING

24

A Marriage Made in Heaven

IN MANY WAYS, Isaac and Rebekah's marriage reads like a fairy tale. One day Rebekah wakes up and discovers that the glass slipper fits. Her kind gesture to a stranger suddenly transforms her from a watering girl into the bride-to-be of a rich, important man. Now it's time to run off and marry him.

There's just one small catch. She's never met him.

Isaac and Rebekah's love story is full of such intriguing twists. God (through an angel) plays matchmaker on the father's behalf, while a servant does the courting. Not a single word is recorded between the lovers, yet the word "love" is used romantically here for the first time in the Bible—"So she became his wife, and he loved her" (Genesis 24:67).

Naturally, Rebekah and Isaac both had to put extraordinary faith in God's matchmaking abilities. What if the servant had returned with a woman Isaac couldn't imagine being intimate with? And how could Rebekah know what life would bring her with an unknown man in a foreign land?

Isaac and Rebekah's example encourages us to be brave for love—to wait patiently; to cross deserts, leaving behind what is easy and familiar; to take risks to truly know our mates; and above all to have faith that God is the gentle keeper of our heart's desires.

Genesis reveals that Isaac and Rebekah went on to have struggles in their marriage, mostly over their children. This doesn't mean they were wrong for each other. It simply reminds us that even a marriage "made in heaven" must be lived out day-by-day on earth—with and in spite of our human shortcomings.

How encouraging to know that God is not only a matchmaker but a *marriage maker*. He has promised "I will be with you always," traveling with us on those journeys over the horizon that love requires. ✍

"*Even a marriage 'made in heaven' must be lived out day-by-day on earth.*"

JACOB&RACHEL
Love Is a Sweet Labor

Place me like a seal over your heart,

like a seal on your arm;

for love is as strong as death,

its jealousy unyielding as the grave.

It burns like blazing fire,

like a mighty flame.

Many waters cannot quench love;

rivers cannot wash it away.

If one were to give

all the wealth of his house for love,

it would be utterly scorned.

Song of Songs 8:6,7

"Many waters cannot quench Love; rivers cannot wash it away."

JACOB&RACHEL

The Marriage:
Granted by Rachel's father
in exchange for 14 years
of Jacob's service.

Children:
Joseph and Benjamin.

Most Memorable Scene:
Jacob breaking into tears
of recognition at the well,
then kissing Rachel.

Greatest Obstacle:
The father-in-law,
who tricked Jacob into
marrying Rachel's sister first.

Compatibility:
Assumed to be good,
since Jacob adored Rachel, yet Rachel's
spiritual commitment is uncertain.

His thoughts were filled with only Rachel

28

ABOUT HIM

Name:
Jacob, "Heel-grabber"
(later changed to Israel, "prince").

Age:
Around 40 at time of marriage.

Appearance:
Unknown.

Personality:
Resourceful and hardworking
with a deeply spiritual and
emotionally vulnerable side.

Family Background:
Parents were Isaac and Rebekah;
twin brother was Esau.

Place in History:
The father of the 12 tribes of Israel.

ABOUT HER

Name:
Rachel, "lamb."

Age:
Probably 20 at the time of marriage.

Appearance:
"Lovely in form, and beautiful."

Personality:
Apparently bright, determined,
and competitive.

Family Background:
Her father was Laban,
Rebekah's brother.

Place in History:
Favored second wife of Jacob;
mother of Benjamin and Joseph.

*Every star in the night sky
was an exciting promise
for their future*

Love Is a Sweet Labor
GENESIS 29

So Jacob served

seven years to

get Rachel,

but they seemed

GENESIS 29:20

like only a few

days to him

because of his

love for her.

He had just walked up to a well in the spring sunshine when he saw her for the first time. She came toward him, surrounded on all sides by woolly waves of sheep bleating their way toward water. Even at a distance, the shepherd girl caught Jacob's attention. His long journey from Canaan—he was about to discover—was over.

Two other shepherds stretched out in the shade of a nearby tree. They watched the girl too. They told Jacob they were all from Haran, but they were waiting for more men to arrive before they tried to move the heavy stone lid from the well.

Jacob turned to the shepherds. "Do you know a man named Laban then?"

"Of course," one replied. He rose on one elbow to nod toward the shepherdess approaching. "The pretty one there is Laban's daughter. Her name is Rachel."

By then she had arrived, giving the men a casual greeting. Jacob could see that the girl had large, beautiful eyes and a lovely figure. With hardly a hesitation, Jacob bounded over to the well, wrapped his arms around the massive stone lid—and heaved. With a terrible grinding, it slid to one side.

And then Jacob set himself to watering Rachel's flock, pulling up gourd after gourd of water and spilling it into the watering troughs. Rachel and the other shepherds watched the energetic stranger, fascinated.

As the gourd rose and fell, Jacob thought of his long journey from Canaan to this place, the land of his ancestors. And he remembered the strange dream he'd had on the way of angels ascending and descending a stairway to heaven, and God's promise to him in that dream—*"I will bless you and watch over you wherever you go."*

Yes, God was watching him now. . . .

When the last sheep was watered, Jacob finally introduced himself to Rachel. By now he was trembling with both fatigue and excitement. "I am

Jacob, your cousin! I am the son of Rebekah, your father Laban's sister!" he nearly shouted. The two of them returned wide-eyed gazes.

THEN JACOB HUGGED RACHEL AND KISSED HER—and abruptly dissolved in a storm of tears. Embarrassed, he wondered if Rachel, too, had grown up hearing countless retellings of how Rebekah had watered the camels of a stranger from Canaan, only to be swept away in a marriage proposal.

But Rachel didn't wait to talk about anything. Instead, she turned and ran for home. So soon she fled, Jacob thought, smiling—exactly like her aunt long ago.

And again it was Laban—this time 60 years older—who went back to the well with the family greeting.

When the two men met, Laban embraced Jacob. "You are my flesh and blood," he said, clapping his nephew on the back. "Come home, please. . . ."

And so Jacob came to stay with his Uncle Laban's family. He spent many hours telling them about Rebekah and his family back home. And day by day, Jacob fell more deeply in love with his cousin, Rachel. Laban's other daughter, Leah, was pretty in her own way—kind, polite, and capable. But there was never a question. Jacob's heart sang only the name of Rachel.

After a month, Laban said to Jacob, "You can't work for me for free just because you're a relative. What do you want for wages?"

Here was Jacob's opportunity. He'd rehearsed this moment in his head but still he hesitated. Jacob wanted Rachel more than he'd ever wanted anything, even more than he'd wanted his father's blessing and the family birthright. But for the first time in his life, Jacob had no tricks up his sleeve and nothing to offer. Except himself.

"Please, my uncle, allow me to work for you seven years without pay in exchange for your daughter Rachel."

31

When Laban accepted his offer, Jacob was so happy he thought he'd never feel the ground beneath him again. What were seven years compared to spending the rest of his life with Rachel?

What's more, Rachel was a bride from the right family—unlike the wives his foolish brother Esau had married. His parents would be pleased.

And so Jacob and Rachel began their courtship under the watchful eye of Laban, secure in their betrothal. A mere glance or smile kept them close, a tender gesture, a wisp of conversation. As was proper, Rachel lowered her eyes in Jacob's presence, and they never touched.

For seven years.

Seven years of sweat and dirt, flies and ticks, stinking goats and stubborn sheep, summer heat and winter cold. But Jacob hardly noticed. His thoughts were filled with only Rachel. Every lamb he carried in the field was Rachel. Every star in the night sky was an exciting promise for their future.

And seven years seemed to him like only a few days. . . .

Until they were up. And then time stood still and the hills seemed to shout, "Seven years are over! The time of marrying has come!"

Jacob went to Laban and said, "Seven years have passed. As I promised, I have worked for you in exchange for your daughter, Rachel. Now let me marry her."

Laban agreed, and the family began to plan the wedding celebration, inviting everyone they knew to celebrate with them.

On the first day of the wedding, Jacob thought Rachel looked more beautiful—even behind her veil—than she had when he first saw her by the well. As the festivities rolled happily along, he hardly heard the music, or noticed the dancing, or listened to the laughter of the wedding guests, so sick was he with love and anticipation.

THAT NIGHT AS HE WAITED IN THE BRIDAL CHAMBER, Jacob felt as if he were in the grip of a dream, as though the sweat and dust of all his years of work had turned into something more beautiful than gold, and he was about to run his fingers through it. Then a curtain parted, and his bride slipped into the darkened room.

"...he hardly heard the music, or noticed the dancing, so sick was he with love and anticipation."

"My heart is gladder than all of these because my love has come to me."

CHRISTINA ROSSETTI

In the morning, he woke up slowly, and before he even opened his eyes, he smiled. Had it really happened? Yes! He had finally married his beloved—

He sat up with a bolt. His head swam with confusion. What was Leah doing in the room? *Their* room? And why was she dressing?

"Leah!" he cried. She turned around to face him, her lower lip trembling. But before she could answer, he knew. Suddenly, he knew. Horror filled him. Laban had not given him Rachel as he promised, but her older sister in her place!

When Jacob confronted him, Laban seemed almost calm. "It is not our tradition to marry the younger daughter before the older," his father-in-law said. "When I said yes, I assumed that Leah would be married off before the seven years were up. But since she is not, she is yours. And I charge you to treat her well!"

Jacob raged. He wanted to break Laban in half with his bare hands. "How could you deceive me this way? You stole from me what was mine! You promised me Rachel! You must give me my wife!"

"I will give you Rachel," answered Laban, stepping back. "But first—out of respect for the bride—you must finish the marriage week with Leah. And in all fairness, since I am giving you *both* of my daughters, you must stay and work another seven years for Rachel."

JACOB COULD HARDLY BELIEVE HIS EARS. The injustice! The treachery! How could he stay and work for a man who had played such a cruel trick on him? He reeled with humiliation.

Love IN BIBLE TIMES

More Than One Wife

During Old Testament times, taking more than one wife was an accepted practice among men who could afford to do so. Many men, kings in particular, also kept a concubine or two. A concubine was a publicly acknowledged mistress (Solomon and Xerxes had hundreds). Often, concubines or multiple wives came as gifts acquired in a political alliance or as the spoils of war.

Israel was surrounded by nations who practiced polygamy. Often, taking extra wives, maids, or concubines to bear children was viewed as a practical means of surviving and prospering. Infant mortality rates were high, and a man with no children had no social security for his old age.

But whether for pleasure or prosperity, multiple wives came at a cost. Interestingly, the Hebrew word for second wife means "rival" or "hostile" (besides Rachel and Leah, consider the stories of Sarah and Hagar, and Hannah and Penninah). And while Jewish law provided guidelines for multiple wives and concubines, the Bible as a whole clearly portrays a one-woman marriage as God's intention (see Genesis 2:24, Matthew 19:6, Mark 10:8, and 1 Timothy 3:12).

Then he weighed his choices. He could turn down Laban's offer and leave with Leah. No one would fault him. Leah would be a good, decent wife. Yet without Rachel, where would he find the heart for living?

But then he remembered God's promise in the dream—"*I will bless you and watch over you wherever you go . . .*"

"I will work another seven years for Rachel," he told his uncle.

The wedding for Jacob and Rachel was put together quickly. News had spread of Laban's trick, and the curious couldn't stay away. They'd never heard of such cold-hearted deception—and from inside one's own family! And the sister, Leah, they wondered—did she plot with her father to take her sister's place?

Yet when the second wedding at Laban's house was over, and the guests went home, what lingered was not the father's incredible deception, but the son-in-law's remarkable love. "Did you see those two looking at each other . . . so happy, so confident?" they mused. "If ever love was worth fourteen years of labor, Jacob and Rachel's is that love!"

In the seven years ahead, while Jacob worked to earn Rachel a second time, he became wealthy from hard work and shrewd dealings. God blessed him with children through both wives—12 sons (the future 12 tribes of Israel) were born to him.

Finally, the young man who had left Canaan years earlier as a fugitive returned, surrounded by flocks, servants, and a large and boisterous family. Jacob had learned that God's promises are stronger than the power of deception to destroy.

Not long after Jacob's clan had returned, Rachel died during her second childbirth. But Jacob's love for her endured the rest of his days. Like at their first encounter by the well, this beautiful girl had turned to go too soon, and taken his heart with her. ❦

"Did you see those two looking at each other... so happy, so confident?"

Love at Twice the Price

JACOB KNEW how to weasel wealth or manipulate circumstances to get his way. But love—love he had to work for. And just when Jacob thought he knew exactly what love would cost him, the price doubled.

We never know when—or even how many times a day—we'll be required to put our personal price tag on love. Who of us hasn't reached a point in our love relationship when the price of commitment suddenly seems to sky rocket? Everything gets more challenging than we ever expected.

But maybe at those very moments, God has something bigger in mind. Maybe, for example, he is inviting us to see past the price tag of love to its value. Costly love can bring new meaning to the simplest act, both for the one giving and the one receiving. Then sweet declarations like "You mean the world to me" or "You're all I'll ever want" turn into life-changing promises. They shine like diamonds on a ring.

Only when Jacob chose to pay twice for Rachel did he start getting his money's worth from love. For the first time, Jacob looked away from getting what he deserved and reached toward what he could offer. Through seven more years of opportunities for second looks and second thoughts, Jacob never wavered. Imagine how valuable Rachel must have felt to know that Jacob wanted to marry her this much!

How much is true love worth, anyway? Solomon would tell us, "If one were to give all the wealth in his house for love, it would be utterly scorned" (Song of Songs 8:7). And Jacob might peer intensely into our eyes and declare, "If you want to know what true love is worth, set the highest price possible—then go twice as far."

"Costly love can bring new meaning to the simplest act, both for the one giving and the one receiving."

BOAZ&RUTH
Love Is a Timely Redemption

My lover spoke and said to me,

"Arise, my darling,

my beautiful one, and come with me.

See! The winter is past;

the rains are over and gone.

Flowers appear on the earth;

the season of singing has come,

the cooing of doves

is heard in our land.

The fig tree forms its early fruit,

the blossoming vines spread their fragrance.

Arise, come, my darling;

my beautiful one, come with me."

Song of Songs 2:10-13

"Arise my darling, my beautiful one, and come with me."

BOAZ & RUTH

The Marriage:
"Proposed" by Ruth in keeping with
a special custom for widows.

Children:
One son, Obed.

Most Memorable Scene:
Ruth approaching Boaz on the
threshing floor as he slept.

Greatest Obstacle:
Ruth was a foreigner;
Boaz was not first in line legally to claim her.

Compatibility:
Apparently excellent; both partners
were honorable, kind, and loyal.

How beautiful you

ABOUT HER

Name :
Ruth, "friendship."

Age:
About 30 at time of
marriage to Boaz.

Appearance:
Jewish tradition says
she was beautiful.

Personality:
Loyal, hard-working, sincere, brave.

Family Background:
From the neighboring country of
Moab, traditional enemy of Israel.

Place in History:
Famous for her loyalty to
her mother-in-law, Naomi.

ABOUT HIM

Name:
Boaz, "in him is strength."

Age:
About 50 at marriage.

Appearance:
Mature, probably graying.

Personality:
Loyal, fair, generous,
honorable, optimistic.

Family Background:
From the tribe of Judah;
an ancestor of Christ.

Place in History:
Obed, his son by Ruth, became the
father of Jesse and the grandfather
of King David.

are
how pleasing. . .

Love Is a Timely Redemption
The Book of Ruth

SMALL BEADS OF PERSPIRATION FORMED on Ruth's temple as she bent to gather the scattered stalks of grain. Her mother-in-law, Naomi, had been right. Gleaning was hot, hard work. But what else could she do? She and her mother-in-law must eat, and Ruth was not too proud to beg.

When Naomi's husband and her two sons had died back in Moab, Naomi had discouraged Ruth from following her here to Bethlehem. "You needn't come with me," she had insisted. "You will be a foreigner. How will you find a new husband? I don't have any more sons for you to marry, and even if I did, you couldn't wait for them to grow up."

But Ruth had clung to Naomi and pleaded with her not to send her away. *"Where you go, I will go, and where you stay, I will stay. Your people will be my people and your God my God"* (Ruth 1:16).

And so far as a new husband. . . . Well, Ruth had decided she would simply not hope for that.

Now, as Ruth labored alone in the scorching heat, she wondered if she'd done the right thing. Was she foolish to have felt so loyal to Naomi? Yesterday, she had heard some of Naomi's friends saying how silly it was for Naomi's childless, widowed daughter-in-law to follow her here. And a Moabitess at that! Who would want to marry such a woman?

That afternoon, the owner of the field Ruth was gleaning in came by to greet the harvesters. His name was Boaz. Ruth could tell right away that he was well liked by the workers. "May the Lord bless you!" he called out to them.

"And may the Lord bless you!" they returned.

A short time later, Ruth was startled when Boaz approached her out in the fields. She noticed that although he wasn't a young man, he had a sturdy build that suggested he was strong and healthy. His dark hair and beard shimmered with threads of silver in the sun.

Boaz greeted her, "Listen carefully, my daughter. Do not go to another field to glean. I like having you here in my fields. And I've told the servants not to bother you in any way. If you get thirsty, feel free to drink from the same jug the servants use."

Ruth was startled. Bowing before him, she asked, "Why are you being so kind to me, especially since I am a foreigner?"

"I have heard about you, Ruth," Boaz answered. His smile flashed kindly while he spoke. *I have been told all about what you have done for your mother-in-law since the death of your husband—how you left your father and mother and your homeland and came to live with a people you did not know before. May the Lord repay you for what you have done. May you be richly rewarded by the Lord, the God of Israel, under whose wings you have come to take refuge* (Ruth 2:11,12).

Ruth thanked Boaz profusely for his blessing, and then he asked her to join the harvesters for their meal. When she was finished, as she prepared to return to work, she overheard Boaz directing the reapers, "I want you to purposely leave plenty of grain for that woman to gather."

THAT NIGHT, RUTH GREETED NAOMI with a flushed face and excitement in her usually calm voice. After she explained how well she had been treated, Naomi asked, "Well, whose field was this?"

"His name is Boaz," said Ruth.

"Why, I know Boaz!" exclaimed Naomi. "He is a relative of Elimelech's, and a kinsman-redeemer of ours. And obviously, he has not forgotten us!"

And so, each day, Ruth went and gleaned in whatever field Boaz's harvesters were working in. And every night, she came home with plenty of grain, and plenty of good things to say about Boaz.

"Do you care for him?" Naomi asked one night.

"But one man loved the pilgrim soul in you..."

W. B. Yeats

Ruth was not given to the kind of giggling and swooning she'd seen some girls practice. But she smiled and blushed. "He is kind to me. . . . He . . . He provides for us . . . He is a good man." And then she added, in case Naomi was forgetting, "I am a Moabitess, an enemy of his people, after all. . . ." But Naomi didn't seem to hear Ruth's last comment. And one night a few weeks later, Naomi sat Ruth down and said to her, "My daughter, don't you think I should try to find a husband for you, a home where you will be well provided for?"

Ruth didn't answer, but she thought she knew what was coming next.

Naomi continued, "As you know, Boaz, whose servant girls you have been gleaning with, is a kinsman with the right to redeem us. And tonight is a perfect time to approach him."

"Tonight?" Suddenly Ruth felt weak.

"I want you to wash and perfume yourself, and put on your best clothes. Then go down to the threshing floor, but don't let Boaz know you are there until he lies down. Then, go and uncover his feet and lie down. He'll tell you what to do."

Ruth hesitated for a moment. And then she answered, "I will do whatever you ask."

"I WILL DO WHATEVER YOU ASK."

That night, Ruth went down to the threshing floor. For some time, she watched Boaz eating and drinking with his harvesting crew. He was very good-natured with them. But then, Ruth had noticed that Boaz was almost always in good humor.

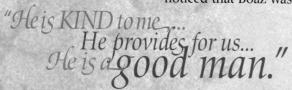

"He is KIND to me... He provides for us... He is a good man."

42

Finally, Boaz went over to lie down at the far end of the grain pile. It was his custom to sleep at the threshing floor during barley season in order to guard his harvest. Besides, the piles of discarded stalks matched any bed for comfort. After he was asleep, Ruth approached him, her heart pounding in her ears. Silently, carefully, she uncovered his feet and lay down.

Her thoughts were troubled. Boaz might not want her. He might even become angry. Why would he want to redeem her, a poor Moabitess, especially when she could probably offer him no children? Surely by now Boaz knew that she'd been married to Naomi's son for ten years without becoming pregnant.

HOURS LATER, BOAZ AWOKE WITH A START and discovered Ruth lying at his feet. "Who are you?" he asked.

Fear clutched Ruth's throat. "I am your servant Ruth," she said just above a whisper. "Spread the corner of your garment over me, since you are a kinsman-redeemer."

She watched the face of Boaz for his reaction.

He broke into a wide smile that shone brightly even in the dim light. "The Lord bless you, my daughter!" Boaz exclaimed. *"This kindness is greater than that which you showed earlier: You have not run after the younger men, whether rich or poor. And now, my daughter, don't be afraid. I will do for you all you ask"* (Ruth 3:10,11).

And then, seeing that Ruth was trembling, Boaz reassured her further. "Everyone knows that you are a woman of great integrity," he said. But then he paused. "However . . ." His voice trailed off momentarily, and Ruth caught her breath.

"There is another man," Boaz continued. "A closer relative than myself, who has the right to redeem you first. Stay here for the night," he told her, "and in the morning if he wants to redeem you, he may. But if he is not willing, I promise you before the Lord that I will."

Love IN BIBLE TIMES

"My Kinsman Redeemer…"

While it's hard for many of us today to imagine marrying our husband's brother, the Hebrew law prescribed just that.

The practice is described in Deuteronomy 25:5,6. If a married man were to die without a son, one of his brothers was to marry the widow and bear children who would carry on the dead brother's name. The kinsman was to "redeem"—buy back—any of the deceased man's property as well, which the first-born son would then inherit.

Ruth's famous request for Boaz to cover her with his garment was a moving appeal for such redemption. "Include me in your marriage bed," Ruth was saying. "Cover me with your family name."

Originally the kinsman marriage applied only to brothers. But by Ruth's time, it was extended to include any close male relative. Considering what might happen in the future, to give a brother or cousin friendly advice on his choice of a wife must have been a serious matter, indeed!

Through the kinsman tradition, God provided for widows, guaranteeing them a future when they had none—and giving us yet another picture of the loving redemption He offers each of us.

"THE LORD BLESS YOU, *My Daughter.*"

So Ruth lay there all night at his feet, never sleeping. In the morning, before anyone might see her, she got up and hurried home.

As soon as Ruth walked in, her mother-in-law delivered a tumult of questions. "How did it go, my daughter? What happened? What did Boaz say?"

Ruth recounted for her every detail of the night from beginning to end. Naomi's weathered face creased with smile after smile. It was all very good news. "My dear Ruth, you won't have to wait long," she said. "Boaz will settle this matter today—you'll see!"

And she was exactly right. Soon word came that the other relative had given Boaz permission to redeem Ruth. The news made Ruth feel both happy and stunned. Only yesterday, she had not dared to hope for a husband!

Boaz and Ruth were married as soon as arrangements could be made. God blessed Ruth with a baby boy. It was hard to tell who was happier about the birth of baby Obed—Naomi or Ruth!

But as Naomi's friends gathered around her to pronounce blessings, Ruth couldn't imagine a greater joy than giving Naomi a grandson. For it was through Naomi's God that she'd obtained a timely redemption—and found a home for her pilgrim heart. ✍

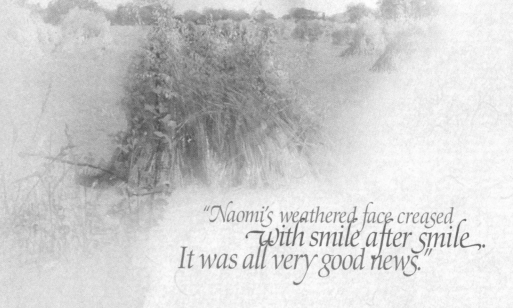

"Naomi's weathered face creased with smile after smile. It was all very good news."

MEDITATION
for Married Lovers

The Romance of Redemption

THE MARRIAGE OF BOAZ AND RUTH is one of the most powerful love stories in the Bible. Yet, amazingly, the word "love" never appears. Perhaps because it doesn't need to.

The setting for Ruth's proposal wasn't exactly romantic. A threshing floor, perhaps even a community one. Boaz's answer might not seem romantic either: "First, I need to make sure this other guy in town doesn't want you." But love, in this case, had little to do with romance—and everything to do with redemption.

As Ruth's kinsman-redeemer, Boaz was fulfilling a legal duty when he married her. But Boaz went much farther than even this. Before she ever asked, Boaz redeemed Ruth—made up for what she lacked—by providing for her, protecting her, and affirming her character.

All of us enter our marriages with some kind of poverty—a broken past, a spiritual hunger, an aching need that went unmet in childhood. Sometimes life can leave us trembling, like Ruth, at our mate's feet. We feel naked and ridiculous. We wonder what we're worth. *When I beg for covering, will I be claimed or rejected?*

This is the exact moment God waits for—when one lover is brave enough to say, "I need you, and it will cost you something." And when the other lover is willing to do whatever it takes to "buy back" and complete the other. *I see who you are—and who you are not—and I still want you!*

Such timely redemption in marriage is our gift of God's grace to each other. And it is also our greatest duty—not to a law, but to love. ❧

"I see who you are—
and who you are not
—and I still want you!"

SAMSON&DELILAH
Love Is a Secret Strength

His arms are rods of gold
set with chrysolite.
His body is like polished ivory
decorated with sapphires.
His legs are pillars of marble,
set on bases of pure gold.
His appearance is like Lebanon,
choice as its cedars.
His mouth is sweetness itself;
he is altogether lovely.
This is my lover...
O daughters of Jerusalem.

Song of Songs 5:14-16

"His body is like polished ivory. He is altogether lovely."

SAMSON&DELILAH   ABOUT HIM

The Marriage:
Lovers who never married.

Children:
None.

Most Memorable Scene:
Delilah lulling Samson to sleep
on her lap while his enemies
hide in the next room.

Greatest Obstacle:
Delilah's selfishness;
Samson's foolishness.

Compatibility:
Low; neither partner
seemed to truly value the other.

Name:
Samson, "sun" or "brightness."

Age:
About 40.

Appearance:
Long hair worn in seven braids,
bulky, muscular form.

Personality:
Charming, brave, rebellious,
vengeful, a womanizer.

Family Background:
His father, Manoah,
was from the tribe of Dan.

Place in History:
Israel's judge and strong-man
who personally helped to deliver
his people from the Philistines.

He always won. And

ABOUT HER

Name:
Delilah, "dainty one."

Age:
Probably around 20.

Appearance:
Traditionally attractive and beguiling.

Personality:
Greedy, self-centered, manipulative.

Family Background:
A Philistine from the Valley of Sorek.

Place in History:
Famous as the woman who extracted the secret of Samson's strength, then betrayed him to the Philistines.

"Let me into your heart, my lover."

now that he was in love he was determined to win Delilah's heart...

Love Is a Secret Strength

JUDGES 16

Samson was in love—again. Her name was Delilah, and she was a tantalizing beauty from the wine country of Philistia. This wasn't the first time Samson had swooned for a foreign temptress. He'd been engaged once already to a sweet girl from Gaza. But the marriage had never been consummated, and the wedding had ended tragically.

Now Samson lay with his head on Delilah's perfumed lap. As her fragrances filled his mind, memories from his youth also drifted through. Winning battles with only a donkey's jawbone for a weapon . . . lions, foxes, and honey . . . the young fiancée who had betrayed his secret to enemies. . . .

She had been a Philistine too. Something about these foreign girls aroused him. They were more interesting somehow, wilder. How could a Hebrew woman match them for excitement?

Of course, his parents had voiced disapproval from the start. "How can you deliver us from our enemies if you marry them?" they said. But how could Samson have known that the girl he loved so much would betray him?

In the nearly 20 years since then, Samson had remained unmarried. He had led Israel as a Nazirite judge—set apart from birth for God's service. But he continued to visit Philistine girls.

Now Delilah's hands stroked Samson's hair, which fell in thick braids to the floor. These days, no one told him who he should marry, or who he should sleep with. From the Jordan River in the east to the Great Sea in the west, Samson knew that no one was more powerful or feared. He always won. And now that he was in love again, he was determined to win Delilah's heart. . . .

That night while Samson slept, the Philistine leaders came to Delilah with a proposal. Samson's capture was worth a lot of money to them. If Delilah could discover the secret of his strength, they would each pay her 1,100 shekels of silver. She'd be rich for life.

Several nights later, she casually questioned Samson. "What makes you so strong, Samson? Are you really invincible?"

A flicker of doubt crossed Samson's mind, but he only smiled, and stroked Delilah's arm. "Sweet Delilah, I'll tell you," he said easily. "If you bind me with seven new leather bowstrings that haven't even dried yet, I'll become as weak as any man."

When Delilah told the Philistines Samson's secret the next day, they brought Delilah seven fresh bowstrings. That night while Samson slept, she bound him hand and foot. The Philistines hid in the next room to see what would happen. But when Delilah playfully yelled, "Samson, the Philistines are upon you!" he sent the leather cords flying. The men in the next room slipped away into the night.

"He liked the look on Delilah's face when she asked him about his great strength..."

Samson burst out laughing at his little trick, but Delilah chided him, "So, you treat me like a fool? You lie to me. . . ?" Then she smiled forgivingly. "Come on, now. It's just me. Tell me how you can be tied."

"YOU REALLY WANT TO KNOW MY SWEET, DON'T YOU?" Samson said. He liked the look on Delilah's face when she asked him about his great strength or plied him with questions about his heroics.

So the next time Delilah pestered him about his secret, Samson prolonged their game. This time he told her to use brand new ropes to tie him up. That night, Delilah again summoned the Philistines, who hid to see what would happen. But like before, Samson snapped off the ropes as if they were threads.

Delilah fumed. "Samson you make such a fool of me! I am so hurt!"

Samson was puzzled when Delilah continued to brood. The subject didn't come up again for some time. But Samson returned to Delilah's door often, drawn back by her charms.

One night when Samson seemed in an especially good mood, and was wanting her to sleep with him, Delilah tried again. "So, my big, brave boy, tell me about your amazing powers. Don't lie this time like before. Let me into your heart, my lover."

Won't she ever give up? thought Samson. These games wore him out. And last time, his trick had made her angry. Besides, he was running out of creative ideas. This time he edged closer to the truth. "OK, this is the real secret of my strength. It has to do with my hair," he said. "If you weave my seven braids onto fabric and pin them tight in a loom, I'll become as weak as any other man."

Samson went to sleep knowing what would happen. And it did. This time when he was awakened with a start, shreds of fabric and splinters of the loom careened around the room.

"That's three times, Samson!" Delilah shouted, bursting into angry tears. "How can you say you love me? You won't even confide in me!"

For a moment, the tears on her cheeks reminded Samson of his bride. Those familiar words echoed painfully. *You hate me! You don't really love me or you would confide in me!*

Could it be that Delilah would betray his secret to his enemies the way his bride had done? Maybe this was no love game at all.

Then again, Samson wondered, maybe Delilah was right—if he couldn't trust her, who could he trust?

From that moment on, Delilah nagged at Samson continually. The question of "The Secret" seemed to consume every minute of their time together. Somehow, Delilah had turned his secret into her strength. How could he possibly make things better between them without telling her the truth? He would have to choose. He

"*He remembered the pain of losing at love...*"

remembered the pain of losing at love, but he couldn't remember losing even one physical contest.

Finally, Samson told her the truth.

"I have been a Nazirite, set apart to God, since birth," he began. "As a sign, no razor has ever been used on my head. If my head were shaved, my strength would leave me, and I would become as weak as any other man."

THERE. IT WAS OVER. HE HAD TOLD HER his precious secret. Delilah would be happy now.

And she was. At her first opportunity, Delilah sent word to the Philistine rulers. "Come tonight. This time he has told me everything, I promise. A woman knows these things. . . . "

That night, to the reassurances of Delilah's admiring gazes and the cool touch of her fingers, Samson dozed off in her arms. He seemed more restless than usual, but finally slept.

Delilah signaled a Philistine to enter the room. As he put a razor to Samson's hair, thick locks fell to the floor one by one. While they fell, Samson seemed to sink ever deeper into his sleep.

This time, when Delilah shouted, "Samson! The Philistines are upon you!" they really were. Samson roused himself, thinking he would shake them free. But his arms and legs felt like lead. He could barely move. The strength God had given him was gone.

Within minutes, mighty Samson was tied up like a heifer. The last thing Samson saw was his enemies giving bags of silver to his lover. Then his captors dragged the judge of all Israel out into the street and gouged out his eyes.

The next day they shackled him and took him to the prison in Gaza. There, they harnessed him to a stone wheel and left him to grind grain day after day.

"*Tell me more, are women true?*"

JOHN FLETCHER

Some time later, the lords and war chiefs of the Philistines decided to gather their people together to celebrate Samson's capture and to offer sacrifices to their god Dagon in his temple. Thousands came for the great event. They sang a raucous praise to Dagon,

> Our god has delivered our enemy
> into our hands,
> the one who laid waste our land
> and multiplied our slain!

IN A FRENZY, THEY CALLED FOR THE PRISONER Samson to be brought out. *"Make Samson perform for Dagon!"* they shouted. *"Make him try to kill us with a donkey's jawbone!"*

All the rulers of the Philistines were there. The temple was so crowded that three thousand climbed onto the roof to watch Samson being paraded around. Now he was only a blind fool being led on a leash by a boy. But they didn't see that his hair had begun to grow back, or notice when he leaned close to the boy's ear. . . .

With the shouts of the crowds filling the air, Samson asked the boy to let him lean against the two central pillars. When he could feel the smooth pillars in each hand, Samson prayed, *"O Sovereign Lord, remember me. Strengthen me just once more, and let me with one blow get revenge on the Philistines for my two eyes."*

Then with his right hand on one pillar and his left on the other, Samson cried out, "Let me die with the Philistines!"

He pushed with all his might. Before the eyes of the jubilant revelers, the pillars began to crack apart and fall. Laughter turned to screams. The upper balconies gave way, spilling people down into the sacrificial fires below. Finally the entire temple collapsed on itself in a roar of stone, dust, smoke, and death.

The next day a messenger arrived in the wine country of Philistia and stood at the door of Delilah's house. But the young woman who answered informed the messenger that Delilah had been gone for several days. "Some say she went to the celebration at the temple," the girl said, then she lowered her voice. "Others say she left the region altogether. She had money, you know. . . . "

The girl halted in mid-sentence. "Did you have some news to leave for her?"

The messenger shook his head seriously. "No," he said. "I believe the news will reach her wherever she is." ❧

Love That Is Not Love

THIS IS A STORY about what love is not.

The Bible tells us that Samson "fell in love" with Delilah. But Samson's feelings were probably closer to infatuation, desire, or lust. It wasn't until he lost his eyes that Samson began to see— "love" had made him blind to flattery and lies.

Any of us who has been deceived or betrayed by love, or played a fool ourselves, can identify with Samson. We recognize his misspent passion, his vulnerability to stupid choices. And we see how easily our strengths, when taken for granted, can turn us into weaklings.

Most of us don't identify as readily with Delilah. But we, too, are capable of selfishness, manipulation, and other sins against love. How many of us have said, "If you loved me you would . . ."? And how often we have exposed a lover's weakness to ridicule.

Because Samson and Delilah's relationship didn't involve commitment, it was easy for them to mistake strong attraction and pleasure for the real thing. But as their story demonstrates, each was using, rather than loving, the other. And each, by taking too much, ended up with less.

If this is what love is not, how do we know what love *is*?

Imagine how differently Samson and Delilah's story would have turned out if they had followed Paul's straightforward answer: "Love is patient, love is kind. It does not envy, it does not boast, it is not proud. It is not rude, it is not self-seeking, it is not easily angered, it keeps no record of wrongs. Love does not delight in evil but rejoices with the truth. It always protects, always trusts, always hopes, always perseveres" (1 Corinthians 13:4-7).

"It wasn't until he lost his eyes that Samson began to see..."

ELKANAH & HANNAH
Love Is a Daily Tenderness

Let us go early to the vineyards

to see if the vines have budded,

if their blossoms have opened,

and if the pomegranates are in bloom—

there I will give you my love.

The mandrakes send out their fragrance,

and at our door is every delicacy,

both new and old,

that I have stored up for you . . .

Song of Songs 7:12,13

"At our door
is every delicacy.
...I will
give you
my love."

ELKANAH&HANNAH

ABOUT HIM

The Marriage:
Complicated by Elkanah's second wife, Peninnah.

Children:
Six.

Most Memorable Scene:
Elkanah trying to comfort Hannah during the festival at Shiloh.

Greatest Obstacle:
Hannah's early barrenness.

Compatibility:
Excellent; mutually devoted to God.

Name:
Elkanah, "God has possessed."

Age:
Probably late 30s.

Appearance:
Unknown.

Personality:
Patient, gentle, kind, devout.

Family Background:
From the hill country of Ephraim.

Place in History:
Father of the prophet Samuel.

"Elkanah," she said between sobs, *"A woman can't compare with her*

ABOUT HER

Name:
Hannah, "gracious."

Age:
Probably late 20s or early 30s.

Appearance:
Unknown.

Personality:
Passionate, intensely devout,
true to her word.

Family Background:
Unknown.

Place in History:
Mother of the prophet Samuel.

*her longing for children
love for a man!"*

Love Is a Daily Tenderness

1 SAMUEL 1,2

Elkanah her husband would say to her, "Hannah, why are you weeping? Why don't you eat? Why are you downhearted? Don't I mean more to you than ten sons?"

1 SAMUEL 1:8

The way the early morning sun hangs like a veil in the smoke-filled air today sets my heart to remembering. How I miss her! In this worn, familiar courtyard of worship, she gave her best gifts to God. And to me, her husband.

I watch our son, Samuel, going about his priestly duties. The sun catches in gold relief the outline of his tall figure stooping to listen to a child's request. Families are already here for festival worship. But my thoughts are all for she who is no longer here. . . .

Hannah, my Hannah . . . slender, devout. She burned with the kind of certainty that could make a man's caution seem like cowardice. With a raised eyebrow, Hannah could make white-haired elders stumble in mid-sentence. On any day the sound of her singing at the loom could fill my heart with peace. I loved her beyond remedy.

We came here to Shiloh every year to give thank offerings to the Lord. I can see our little family sitting together on these stones while Hannah—newly my wife—sang happily, eyes tightly shut. The smoke of our sacrifices rose along with young Hannah's lilting voice. Later, on the road toward home, her songs of faith followed us like a flock of yellow birds.

But years pass, and sounds change. Our family kept returning here to Shiloh for all the feasts, but increasingly Hannah's praises mingled with petitions and laments of longing. The festivals, meant to be celebrations of God's bounty, became the milestones of her grief. For she was barren. Each year, my other wife Peninnah would bring yet another baby to be dedicated. But Hannah sat with empty arms. I tried to fill them every day with small, tender acts—a kiss, a flower for the table, a walk.

But as our family grew, so did Hannah's emptiness.

Peninnah made things worse. One year, my wives and all the children sat on these stones, waiting for our family's turn at the altar. Peninnah didn't see me standing behind her as she leaned to say something into Hannah's ear. "Here I sit in the midst of my sons and daughters," she murmured in mock glee. "And tell me, Hannah darling, for what bounty do you give thanks this year?"

Hannah didn't answer. She preferred—no, she was certain—that wives in a family should be as faithful to each other as they are to their husband. But Hannah's shoulders began to shudder.

I stepped forward to touch her. "Hannah, sweet one," I asked, "what can I do? How may I comfort you?"

She looked up without speaking. In her wet eyes I saw flames reflected from the sacrificial fire. *Lord God,* I inwardly groaned, *will you let this fire burn her heart to ashes?*

Later, during our sacrificial feast, I gave Peninnah a portion of stewed lamb for her and each of her children. But to Hannah I gave a double portion. I wanted to stand with her in some way, to say, *Yes, I'm certain, too. You'll carry a baby soon.*

That night I found Hannah weeping. "Hannah," I said, taking her in my arms, "please don't weep. Please take something to eat. Why are you so downhearted about this thing? Don't I mean more to you than ten sons?"

"Elkanah, you don't understand," she said between sobs. "A woman can't compare her longing for children with her love for a man!"

WHAT DID I KNOW OF WOMEN THEN? Or know now? When a man loves, he hopes to wipe away each sorrow with a fiercer tenderness. All night Hannah shook in my arms like a reed in the wind.

We trudged home in near silence the next day. Did God care about the heartache of my young wife? With every step, I prayed that he would grant Hannah's pleas for children—or bring our family peace and contentment in some other way. Surely, without his provision, Hannah would never return to Shiloh again.

"Do not think that love in order to be genuine has to be extraordinary. What we need is to love without getting tired."
MOTHER TERESA

But the next year she did. Even Peninnah was surprised. Everything seemed to be going well until the day before we were to leave. As the family feast was drawing to a close, Hannah suddenly stood up—near where I am sitting at this moment—trembling. Bitter tears began pouring down her face. She tottered like a drunk, hands raised to heaven, eyes closed. Soon she began to pray—silently mouthing her petition.

Later, she told me every word of it:

"O Lord Almighty! If you truly see how miserable I am, and if you even remember that I exist, then I ask you to give me a son. And if you do, I will give him back to you. For all the days of his life, he will be your servant!"

Our family watched as Hannah poured out her anguished plea. Eli the priest had also been watching. Now he stepped in front of my distraught wife and shook a finger in her face. "How long will you keep getting drunk?" he scolded, loud enough for all the children to hear. "Go somewhere and rest until the wine leaves your head!"

Startled, Hannah opened her eyes. "No, no, my lord!" she replied, fixing him with her gaze. "I haven't been drinking wine or beer. I'm in utter anguish! I've been praying here to the Lord out of my deep grief. Please, don't assume that I'm a wicked woman. "

Eli realized that he'd been mistaken. And now his tone changed. "Go in peace," he said gently. "And may the God of Israel grant you what you've asked of him."

"May I find favor in your eyes," Hannah said.

Hannah gathered her skirts around her, and sat down among the children. In a few minutes, she was eating, seemingly wrapped in a great calm.

Early the next morning, we worshiped the Lord together, then left for home. For the first time in years, Hannah's songs flitted around us on the way.

On our bed in Ramah, Hannah excitedly told me everything.

She was confident now that God would answer her prayer—and she was already preparing to keep her vow. "Caress me with praise and thanksgiving on every fingertip, Elkanah," she said smiling. She said it with such music in her voice, I couldn't doubt. Or wait.

We made love like a newly married couple—without loneliness, without disappointment. A pure flame of desire burned over our bed, and pure springs of peace watered our souls.

On that very night, or so it seemed to us later, the Lord chose to remember Hannah—her wifely longings and years of pleadings, and the vow she made here in Shiloh.

Hannah conceived. All during her months of budding and swelling, our family was swept up in her joy. It was a balm that brought healing to us all—first to Hannah's wounded heart, then to my hopes, and finally even to resistant Peninnah.

When Hannah gave birth to a beautiful son, she named him Samuel, "Heard of God." Our rejoicing was complete. The echoes of Peninnah's scorn had faded. In Hannah's arms she cradled her heart's desire, and a symbol of our love—a baby of her own.

When a year had passed, and our family was readying to return to Shiloh, Hannah announced she was staying home. I wondered if she was flinching from her promise, but she must have sensed my question. She held my face in her hands. "After Samuel is weaned, I'll take him and present him to the Lord," she said. "And he will live there forever."

"Do what seems best to you," I replied.

Yes, giving the boy to temple service would be keeping our pledge to God. But how could I want the return of loneliness for dear Hannah? What music of God could replace the sound of her own child's laughter?

The year that Samuel was weaned and done with his early

Love IN BIBLE TIMES

One in Spirit

Today we often consider spiritual unity to be the most rewarding kind of intimacy in marriage, and scores of books have been written to help couples achieve it.

But how much spiritual intimacy did biblical couples share?

In Old Testament times, a wife was simply expected to obey her husband in all religious matters. She was welcome to join the three yearly pilgrimages—The Feast of Tabernacles, The Yearly Feast of the Lord, and the Festival of the New Moon—but only her husband was required to go. She could not enter the Temple's inner court, read the Torah herself, or recite prayers in the synagogue, but she could sit and listen in a special section called the "Court of Women."

Elkanah's respect and support for his wife's spiritual decisions—"do what seems best to you" (1 Samuel 1:23)—was highly unusual, as was Hannah's public prayer in the temple. It wasn't until after Christ's ascension that the Bible portrays women praying aloud in public (Acts 12: 1-7, 1 Corinthians 11: 2-16). Jesus was revolutionary when he honored women's spirtual contributions. And Paul may have had Elkanah and Hannah in mind when he told husbands, "Love your wife as your own body..." (Ephesians 5:28).

training, and beginning to spend hours running and jumping with his playmates, Hannah said she was ready for the trip to Shiloh. She had patiently prepared our son for his new life, explaining the privilege of his special calling. She had lovingly sewn him a wardrobe and packed his favorite toys.

We brought offerings to the Lord that year—a three-year-old bull, a large sack of flour, and a skin of wine—but Samuel was the gift that cost us everything.

When we stood with our little boy before Eli in this courtyard, Hannah reminded him who she was. "I'm the very same woman who stood here beside you some years ago, praying to conceive a child," she said. "The Lord has given to me what I asked of him. So now I give him to the Lord. For the rest of his life he will belong to the Lord."

Having said those words and kept her vow, Hannah was overcome as before. But not with grief. This time, the words that rushed to her lips were a song of praise:

> My heart rejoices in the Lord;
> in the Lord my horn is lifted high.
> My mouth boasts over my enemies,
> for I delight in your deliverance.
> There is no one holy like the Lord;
> there is no one besides you;
> there is no Rock like our God.

Each year after that, before we came here for the annual sacrifice, Hannah sewed Samuel a new robe and brought it to him. We watched proudly as our little boy ministered under Eli the priest. And every year when we entered the tabernacle courtyard, Eli would greet me with a blessing:

> May the Lord give you children by this woman
> to take the place of the one she prayed for
> and gave to the Lord!

And He did. While Samuel was growing up in God's service, God remembered Hannah again. And again. Hannah gave birth to three more sons and two daughters....

Now a hand on my shoulder startles me from my remembering.

I look up. It is Samuel, looking into my face—with Hannah's eyes, and his own wise smile. "You are remembering again, Father?"

My son knows the story well enough, the story of his mother and his birth. I know it as the story of an ordinary husband and wife, and a love which survived for many years on mere tokens of hope. Yet today I see how hope has become a certainty, rising like incense on this Shiloh morning. "Yes, Samuel," I answer him. "I am remembering her . . . "

MEDITATION
for Married Lovers

Love Tokens

SCRIPTURE TELLS US little about the romance of Elkanah and Hannah. We don't know anything about their engagement, the occasion of the wedding, or even whether Elkanah considered his young wife beautiful.

What Scripture does provide us with is a record of little deeds and great faith. Clearly, when God took time to share this love story, he wasn't interested in sparks and swooning but in the kind of married love that outlasts life's troubles.

An old saying, "Love is friendship set on fire," seems particularly fitting for this couple. Elkanah's devotion shines through in his sensitivity to Hannah's grief over her childlessness. He could have shamed her for her "inadequacy," or even divorced her. Instead he loved Hannah for *who* she was far more than for *what* she could or could not give him.

And so Elkanah tried to fill her emptiness with gifts of comfort, affirmation, and honor. The extra portion he gave her "because he loved her," sounds trivial. But it was a tender act worthy to be recorded in the Bible for all time.

Nearly every couple experiences deep disappointment together—the loss of a child, chronic illness, financial disaster, unfulfilled goals. When life is not turning out as we hoped, it's easy to focus on what our mate isn't giving us—or can't give us even if he or she wants to.

At such times, small gifts of kindness reassure our mates that we treasure them no matter what. Perhaps Paul had Elkanah in mind when he wrote to the Ephesians, "Be completely humble and gentle; be patient, bearing with one another in love" (Ephesians 4:2). Each day, God invites us to remember that Elkanah was right. Small tokens of love given with great faithfulness make way for God's best miracles.

"Small gifts of kindness reassure our mates that we treasure them no matter what."

DAVID & MICHAL
Love Is a Fragile Trust

My lover is mine and I am his;

he browses among the lilies.

Until the day breaks

and the shadows flee,

turn my lover,

and be like a gazelle

or like a young stag

on the rugged hills....

All night long on my bed

I looked for the one my heart loves;

I looked for him but did not find him.

Song of Songs 2:16–3:1

"My lover is mine and I am his."

DAVID&MICHAL

The Marriage:
Arranged by her father,
King Saul, for the price
of 100 enemy lives.

Children:
None.

Most Memorable Scene:
Michal watching David
dance in ecstasy before
the Ark of the Covenant.

Greatest Obstacle:
Her father's deranged interferences.

Compatibility:
Low; at odds spiritually;
extreme family differences.

ABOUT HER

Name:
Michal, "who is like God?"

Age:
Probably about 15 at time of marriage.

Appearance:
Possibly tall, dark, and striking— like her father.

Personality:
Prideful, concerned with appearances, devoted to David.

Family Background:
Grew up in Israel's first royal family.

Place in History:
The wife who was jealous of her husband's devotion to God.

ABOUT HIM

Name:
David, "beloved."

Age:
Probably about 20 when he married Michal.

Appearance:
Ruddy, handsome, athletic.

Personality:
Emotional, reflective, brave, devoted to God, a leader.

Family Background:
Grew up near Bethlehem, herded sheep as a boy for his father Jesse.

Place in History:
The boy who killed Goliath; the "man after God's own heart"; author of many psalms; Israel's greatest king.

Like a leaf on a summer breeze, the rumor of a princess in love wafted through the halls of the palace

Love Is a Fragile Trust

1 Samuel 18; 2 Samuel 3–6

Now Saul's daughter Michal was in love with

1 Samuel 18:20

David, and when they told Saul about it, he was pleased . . .

Like a leaf on a summer breeze, the rumor of a princess in love wafted through the halls of the palace. The king's daughter, Michal, pined for a young warrior. But not just any warrior. For David, the giant slayer. David, the national darling, the hero of Israel.

But who could be surprised? Michal had felt the pull of David's charm when he first played his harp in court. She had witnessed David's steady loyalty to her temperamental father. She'd stood close to his rugged beauty.

And now suddenly, this daydream of every Israelite girl was within her reach. Out of some quaint humility, David had refused to claim Michal's older sister Merab as his rightful prize for killing Goliath. Her sister was married off to another man, leaving Michal next in line to be given in marriage. The moment had come to let her heart's secret be known . . .

When court attendants cautiously whispered word of Michal's affections to her father, King Saul seemed happy to hear of it. But Michal's hopes sank when she heard about David's response to the king's marriage offer. It was the same as for her older sister: "It would be a great honor, but I'm just a poor man."

Just what kind of prize could get David's attention? This time, King Saul knew the answer. He appealed to David's daring nature. To the one Israelite brave enough to have battled Goliath, the king threw down a seemingly impossible challenge. If David could kill 100 Philistine warriors in an allotted time—and come back with their foreskins as proof—he could claim Michal as his bride.

The strategy worked. David sent back word, "Tell the king that I'd be pleased to become his son-in-law."

Michal was elated to hear that David might want her after all, but her happiness was quickly engulfed by fears for his safety. What if the rumors—that her father was actually trying to kill David—were true? What if he died attempting to win her hand?

No one was more relieved than the lovestruck princess when David and his band of men returned alive from their grisly raid—with time to spare and holding up the bloody proof of 200 enemy dead, twice the number Saul had requested.

And so it came about that on a day soon after, flowers and singing maidens filled the corridors and courtyards of the palace. It was the wedding of the year, and as David stooped to kiss her, Michal felt certain she would never be happier. She was marrying the hero of her dreams, and she was achieving for her father the political alliance of a lifetime . . .

But Michal's joy was short-lived. As time passed, King Saul's hateful suspicions about David became increasingly evident. In fact, the more Michal's feelings for David revealed themselves to be deeper than mere fancy, the more Saul resented his new son-in-law. One day a court insider offered Michal a veiled caution: "Remember, lovely Michal, you are first of all a daughter of the king. Guard your loyalties wisely."

WHEN ANOTHER PHILISTINE WAR BROKE OUT, David again proved successful in battle. Unable to bear the thought of hearing more "David has killed his ten thousands" songs in the streets, Saul's demons of jealousy and fear ran wild. Summoning several trusted men, he ordered them to go to David and Michal's home, watch until dawn, then break in and kill David.

A source close to Saul alerted Michal of the plan, and she acted quickly. "If you don't run for your life," she warned David, "I am sure that tomorrow my father's men will kill you!" She took a life-sized idol, laid it on the bed, and covered it with clothing and goat hair at the head. Then she helped her husband escape through a window, tearfully declaring her love as David lowered himself into the darkness below.

In the morning when Saul's men came up to capture David, Michal motioned toward the figure in bed and said with feigned concern, "David is very sick."

The men believed her, and refused to take the plot further. But when they told Saul what had happened, he was furious. "Bring him here in his bed if you have to," he roared, "and I'll kill him myself!"

The men rushed back to David's house only to discover Michal's trick. When her father discovered what she had done, he summoned her to the palace. "Why did you deceive me like this?"

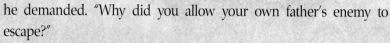

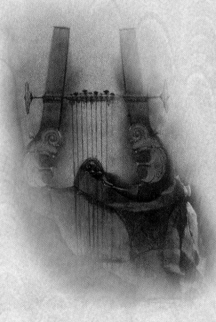

he demanded. "Why did you allow your own father's enemy to escape?"

She wanted to scream, *Because I love him much more than you hate him!* But instead she answered with a well-rehearsed lie. "David threatened me," she said coolly. "He said if I didn't let him escape, he'd kill me."

As Michal walked home, loneliness and a vague sense of doom settled on her spirit. When would she see David again? All she wanted was to be loved by both her father and her husband.

Michal soon learned that David was safe. He was roaming the countryside with his small band of fighters, hiding in caves and deserts. The hero who had saved Israel from the Philistines was now a refugee from his own father-in-law, living off handouts. Weeks turned into months. Months turned into years. Saul continually tried and failed to capture David. Michal waited and hoped. And then one day the unthinkable happened. Her father appeared at her door accompanied by several stone-faced advisers and announced that her marriage to David was over. He had given her in marriage to a man named Paltiel.

For many years, Michal remained Paltiel's hostage-wife. Paltiel was a caring husband. But he was no national hero, and he wasn't her David.

Michal followed closely the news of David's exploits. Year by year, his reputation as a warrior and leader grew. He defeated armies and escaped countless deadly traps while still choosing to respect, and even protect, the king who hunted him. Through it all, David proved he was more than just a boy hero or adventurer. He convinced the nation of what Michal had always known in her heart—David, son of Jesse, was God's chosen heir to her father's throne.

At the same time, she grieved to see a steady decline in her own family's fortunes. Even as enemies pressed in from every side, King Saul's increasingly erratic behavior made him a national joke. Then tragedy struck. Her father's army was defeated in a battle with the Philistines. Three of Michal's brothers were killed, and Saul took his own life rather than be captured by enemy forces.

After Saul's death, David was anointed king of the southern tribes of Israel (the northern tribes continued to be ruled by Saul's family). Michal stopped dreaming of the day when David would come to reclaim her. She heard each time David took another wife or was blessed with yet another son. And each time, a cherished part of her heart seemed to wither like a leaf and blow away . . .

ONE DAY SEVEN YEARS LATER, as David was preparing to become king of a united Israel, Michal received word that he was demanding her return. He sent messengers to one of her brothers, saying, "Remember, I paid for her with the blood of Israel's enemies!"

When King David's men arrived to remove Michal from the home of Paltiel, she felt as if she were moving in a dream. It seemed like only yesterday it had been her father's men at the door. Not even Paltiel's wails of protest could penetrate her spirit, even when he followed the military escort for miles, weeping loudly.

On the road to Jerusalem, Michal wondered what kind of husband, what affections, would await her this time when she walked into David's presence? Once, she had been a princess, the envy of every Hebrew girl. Now her father and brothers were long dead, and her family name was a public disgrace.

Love IN BIBLE TIMES

The Wedding Day

Michal and David's wedding must have been a grand affair. Oxen and fatted calves were killed and roasted. Music and dancing went on into the night. In a royal wedding, no cost was spared.

And unlike weddings of today, it wasn't over in 20 minutes, or even 20 hours. The main event was a reception referred to as the wedding feast that usually lasted anywhere from 7 to 30 days.

Failing to attend a wedding was considered a grave insult. Invitations were delivered twice—one in advance, and one when the party was ready. Festivities couldn't begin, however, until the bridegroom and his attendants went to joyfully escort the bride and her maids to the groom's home, where the wedding took place.

Everyone was expected to dress in their finest attire for the occasion. Brides dressed elaborately, often wearing jeweled tiaras or garlands of fresh flowers, and finely embroidered garments. "Can a maid forget her ornaments, or a bride her attire?" wrote the prophet Jeremiah.

Throughout the celebrations, the couple usually sat under a canopy where friends and family pronounced blessings for a long life and many sons. Just before the party ended, bride and groom were escorted to the nuptial chamber to consummate their marriage.

73

Most painful of all, Michal was certain by now that she was barren.

When she and David finally stood in the same room again, Michal saw how much the years had changed them both. Gone was the happy shepherd boy who had once made her swoon. And faded, she knew, was the bright innocence David had once found in her own face. Now her love for him, if it could be revived, would have to be shared—with other memories and other wives.

Years later, Michal stood at her palace window. Once, she had watched her young husband escaping into the night through their bedroom window. But today she watched a very different scene. On the streets below, a noisy, happy throng followed the Ark of the Covenant as it was carried into the city. The king led the procession, leaping and dancing in worshipful abandon, stripped down to only his loincloth.

She couldn't help noticing how all the young girls watched her king with dazed smiles and something in their eyes that she recognized. Something that made her suddenly and completely despise David in her heart.

When he arrived home, David was jubilant. But Michal met him with disdain. "How amazing you were to watch today!" she said bitingly. "Here was the king himself, taking off his clothes and dancing about so the slave girls could ogle him. You acted like any ordinary fool!"

David was stunned. "I was dancing before the Lord, and not in front of the girls, as you're saying," he replied.

When Michal turned away, David's anger flared. "Why were you not dancing yourself, Michal?" he asked. "Remember that the Lord chose me—not your father or anyone from your family—to be king. So I'll celebrate before Him any way I like! And if I embarrass myself even more for the Lord's sake, these slave girls will continue to honor me."

David went on to become Israel's greatest king. But Michal's silhouette receded from the window of national life, disappearing into the shadows of the harem and of history. She would never bear children. Michal—daughter of Israel's first king and wife of its greatest king—would end her life not in love, but in bitterness.

Wounded Love

THE LOVE STORY of David and Michal unfolds a lot like a Shakespearean tragedy. A scheming king, his love-struck daughter, and the handsome object of her affection all travel toward an inevitable, painful collision.

While David's ascent to the throne is at the center of this drama, the love story really belongs to Michal. How amazing that, in the midst of its record of kings and wars, the Bible slows down to tell us in piercing detail about a young princess whose marriage seemed doomed before it began. Her story begins, "Now Saul's daughter Michal was in love with David. . . ." It ends later with the sad words, "She despised him in her heart."

Scripture tells us *twice* that Michal loved David. And when forced to choose between loyalty to her father and love for her husband, Michal chose David, saving his life in the process. So how did such devotion descend into contempt?

Much of Michal's story turns on events that seem beyond her control: betrayal, trauma, abandonment, separation. We shouldn't be surprised that Michal became bitter. In fact, any of us who has endured similar sorrows can feel compassion for her. As Shakespeare's Romeo put it, "He jests at scars who never felt a wound."

And yet we all know love relationships that endure and even thrive in spite of scheming in-laws, long separations, and the death of loved ones. These husbands and wives have learned what Michal didn't—that the real enemy of a marriage doesn't lie outside of us, but within our own choices and attitudes.

Imagine a different final scene at the window. Michal has forgiven her tortured, abusive father. She sees how, partly through her own extreme sacrifice, God has protected and exalted her David—and through him, her nation. And when she looks down at the king dancing in the streets, she remembers not injustices but a young man who brought her music and laughter in a lonely palace long ago.

Yes, love is a fragile trust. But with God's help, we can guard our hearts against bitterness and reach instead for faith, courage and forgiveness. And this kind of love will never fail (1 Corinthians 13:8).

"With God's help, we can guard our hearts against bitterness."

75

The Rise and Fall of the Bible's Greatest Lover

JUST READ HIS POEMS—collected in the Book of Psalms—and you know that David was a passionate man. He pursued his life and his devotion to God with intensity and sometimes reckless abandon. No surprise then that this man of deep emotion would easily win the title of the Bible's greatest lover.

During his long and colorful life, he married eight wives who are named in Scripture, but he also took other wives and concubines about whom we know nothing. The three women we meet in some detail in the Bible accounts—Michal, Abigail, and Bathsheba—are fascinating personalities themselves, and each shows us David in a different light.

Surely God wanted to tell us something important when he paused to focus on these relationships. ✍

Abigail, a Gift of Destiny

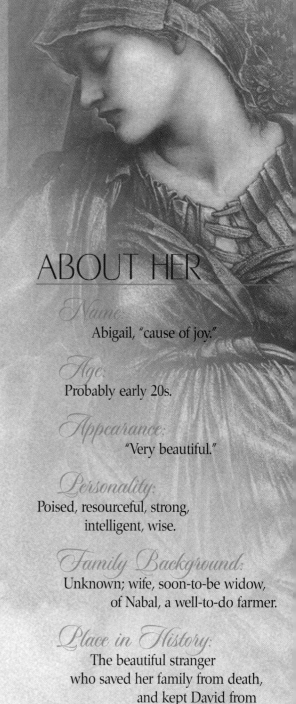

ABIGAIL MET DAVID AT THE LOW POINT of his young life. His father figure and mentor, the prophet Samuel, had just died. David was living like a fugitive in the deserts of southern Judah, on the run from King Saul. And even though David had spared Saul's life during a dramatic encounter, Saul had responded by giving David's wife, Michal, to another man.

During these days of humiliation and hunger, he wrote: *"O God, you are my God, earnestly I seek you … in a dry and weary land where there is no water"* (Psalm 63:1). David must have often wondered if he had any future at all.

One day David sent messengers to ask a wealthy rancher in the region for food for his ragged band of followers. But Nabal was a stingy, ill-tempered drunkard who sent back a stinging reply: "Who is this David? Who is this son of Jesse?"

David's anger flared, and he vowed that no one would be alive at Nabal's estate by morning. Enter Abigail. A hired hand told the young wife about her husband's heartless response, and warned, "Disaster is hanging over our master and his whole household!"

Quickly Abigail and her servants loaded up a caravan with bread, wine, grain, dried fruit, and meat and sent the relief supplies to David's camp. No one breathed a word to Nabal.

Then Abigail herself rode on her donkey to intercept the armed men headed toward her home. Imagine the scene in a desolate canyon when David's band of desert fighters suddenly came upon a poised and beautiful young woman on a donkey: The men come to a halt in confusion and surprise. Dust swirls. Abigail dismounts and walks straight toward their leader.

ABOUT HER

Name:
Abigail, "cause of joy."

Age:
Probably early 20s.

Appearance:
"Very beautiful."

Personality:
Poised, resourceful, strong, intelligent, wise.

Family Background:
Unknown; wife, soon-to-be widow, of Nabal, a well-to-do farmer.

Place in History:
The beautiful stranger who saved her family from death, and kept David from needless bloodshed.

Abigail took advantage of their surprise to deliver a stirring speech to David. Bowing at David's feet, Abigail begged him to blame her for the foolish behavior of her husband. Then she helped him look past the immediate circumstances to what really mattered:

The Lord will certainly make a lasting dynasty for my master, because he fights the Lord's battles. Let no wrongdoing be found in you as long as you live. Even though someone is pursuing you to take your life, the life of my master will be bound securely in the bundle of the living by the Lord (1 Samuel 25:28,29).

When she had presented the gifts of food to David, she reminded him of what was at stake. By turning away from needless bloodshed now, she said, David would have a clean conscience later when the Lord had fulfilled his promises for David's life.

David's reaction was a burst of gratitude. "May the Lord reward you for your good judgment!" he said. Abigail had defused his anger and averted a catastrophe for everyone under her care. After accepting her gifts, David sent Abigail and her servants home in peace.

The next day when Nabal found out what his wife had done, he suffered a heart attack; ten days later he was dead. After the period of mourning was over, David sent several men to Abigail with a request—he wanted the widow of Nabal to become his wife.

Both Michal and Abigail suffered life's injustices. Yet while hardships embittered Michal, they seemed to only deepen Abigail. Both women also delivered the same powerful message to their husband: "Remember, you are a king, so act like a king." Yet where Michal used the words to mock and belittle, Abigail used them to help David believe in his future when his faith was almost gone.

Abigail left the comfort of her estate to face the wilderness with David and his men. She was even taken hostage by enemy raiders for a time. But as loyal wife of God's outlaw and later of God's anointed king, Abigail built a legacy as the noblest of his wives.

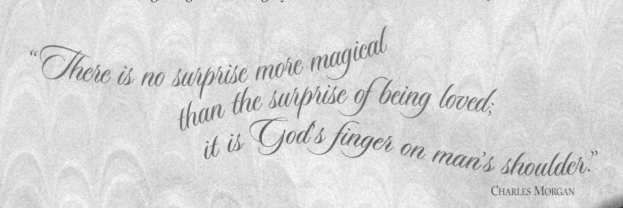

"There is no surprise more magical than the surprise of being loved; it is God's finger on man's shoulder."

Charles Morgan

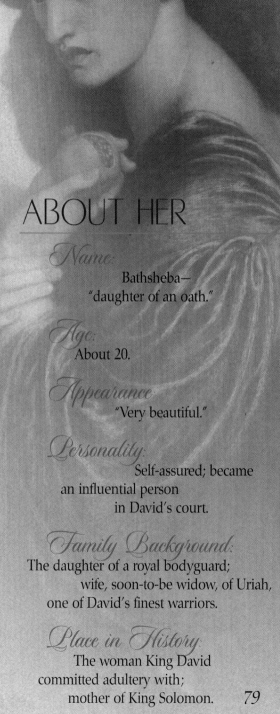

Bathsheba, a Crisis of Conscience

EVEN THOUGH THE BIBLE CALLS DAVID "the man after God's own heart," David's heart led him into a lot of trouble. The story of Bathsheba and David is a favorite "love story" of romance novelists and filmmakers, but like the story of Delilah and Samson, it's really more about weakness and lust than love.

Twenty years had passed since David's fugitive days. Now he had a secure kingdom, a large and stable royal family, and—unfortunately, as it turned out—time to enjoy the fruits of success. One luxury was the freedom to stay home when his armies went off to war.

Walking on the roof of his palace one spring evening, David looked down to see a woman on a nearby rooftop. She was naked, taking a bath. Even from a distance, her astonishing beauty immediately aroused him. With hardly a thought, he sent a messenger to summon her.

Her name was Bathsheba, wife of one of David's own most trusted fighting men, Uriah, who was away at the front. Without protest, Bathsheba obeyed and she spent the night giving the king pleasure in his chambers.

Some time later Bathsheba sent word to David that she was pregnant. David decided a simple cover-up was in order. He sent word to have Uriah returned from the front. After going through the motions of taking a first-hand report on the war effort from Uriah, David told the soldier to go home and relax.

ABOUT HER

Name:
Bathsheba—
"daughter of an oath."

Age:
About 20.

Appearance:
"Very beautiful."

Personality:
Self-assured; became an influential person in David's court.

Family Background:
The daughter of a royal bodyguard; wife, soon-to-be widow, of Uriah, one of David's finest warriors.

Place in History:
The woman King David committed adultery with; mother of King Solomon.

79

But Uriah refused to cooperate with David's plan. How could he enjoy the pleasures of home and wife, he said, when the Ark of the Covenant and all of Israel's fighting men were making do in tents? He slept on the steps of the palace instead. The next night David tried getting Uriah drunk and sending him home, but that didn't work either. The king would have to think of something else.

By the time Uriah left for the front the next day, he was a doomed man. In his pocket, Uriah carried a sealed message from the king for his general. David instructed the general to intentionally position Uriah within range of enemy archers, then retreat so that he would be killed. Within a matter of days, Uriah was dead.

DAVID MARRIED BATHSHEBA as quickly as possible and soon she bore a son. If anyone suspected a conspiracy, no one mentioned it. The couple assumed that an ugly, private sin was behind them—until the day the prophet Nathan strode into court.

Telling a parable about a rich man with many sheep who stole a poor man's only lamb, Nathan confronted King David with his sin. "You are the man!" he declared.

"Why did you despise the word of the Lord by doing what is evil?" asked the prophet. *"This is what the Lord, God of Israel, says: I anointed you king over Israel, and I delivered you from the hand of Saul. I gave your master's house to you, and your master's wives into your arms. I gave you the house of Israel and Judah. And if all this had been too little, I would have given you even more"* (2 Samuel 12:7,8).

Humbled and ashamed, David immediately confessed. Nathan reassured him that his sins of adultery and murder had been forgiven. But other consequences were inescapable. The king's family life would be marked by ongoing calamities. And the child born to David and Bathsheba would die.

As the sound of Nathan's footsteps faded in the palace hallways, David and Bathsheba faced their darkest hour. But despite their sorrows, for the first time their marriage could flourish in God's blessing. David wrote, *"Create in me a pure heart, O God, and renew a steadfast spirit within me. Do not cast me from your presence or take your Holy Spirit from me"* (Psalm 51:10,11).

When the child died, David put aside his grief and comforted Bathsheba. Soon Bathsheba was pregnant again. When another son was born, the couple named him Solomon, "peace."

One day, they heard the prophet's footsteps again. But this time Nathan brought words of hope, not accusation. God wanted David and Bathsheba to know that he loved their new boy, Nathan said. God even had a special name for the baby—Jedidiah, "Loved by the Lord."

As David aged, he showed continuing respect and affection for the queen who had come to him in such terrible circumstances. He kept his promise to her to make Solomon his successor. In his failures with Bathsheba, David had seen the darkness of his own heart, but he had also realized that the love relationship that mattered most to him was the one between himself and his God.

"Love is of all passions the strongest, for it attacks simultaneously the head, the heart, and the senses."

VOLTAIRE

HOSEA & GOMER
Love Is a Costly Way

My dove in the clefts of the rock,

in the hiding places on the mountainside,

show me your face,

let me hear your voice;

for your voice is sweet,

and your face is lovely.

Catch for us the foxes,

the little foxes

that ruin the vineyards,

our vineyards that are in bloom.

Song of Songs 2:14,15

"Show me your face, let me hear your voice; for your voice is sweet and your face is lovely."

The Marriage:
God told Hosea to take Gomer,
a prostitute, as his wife.

Children:
Three.

Most Memorable Scene:
God ordering Hosea to forgive
and take back his straying wife.

Greatest Obstacle:
Gomer's unfaithfulness.

Compatibility:
Extremely low; they had almost
nothing in common.

Name:
Gomer, "complete."

Age:
Probably early 20s.

Appearance:
Possibly quite attractive.

Personality:
Morally weak and disloyal.

Family Background:
Daughter of Diblaim,
a Baal worshiper.

Place in History:
The prostitute who became
the wife of a prophet.

"Two love mine and my Lord's—had
Two hearts had been

ABOUT HIM

Name:
Hosea, "deliverance."

Age:
Unknown.

Appearance:
Unknown.

Personality:
Sensitive to God's heart,
compassionate towards others,
bold, highly principled.

Family Background:
From an upper class family
in the Northern Kingdom of Israel.

Place in History:
Old Testament prophet ordered
to use his marriage as a living
demonstration of how God
felt about Israel's idolatry.

*stories —
somehow become one story
broken in the same place."*

Love Is a Costly Way

The Book of Hosea

The Lord said to me, "Go, show your love to your wife again, though she is loved by another and is an adulteress. Love her as the Lord loves the Israelites, though they turn to other gods. . . ."

Hosea 3:1

MY NAME IS HOSEA, SON OF BEERI. Let me tell you my love story. If you are new to love, you might think my story is ugly, like a baby with a deformity, and should be kept hidden. But if you listen to the end you might understand finally, as I did. . .

I am a street prophet in Samaria, capital of the Northern Kingdom. My calling is to proclaim God's steadfast love to the common people of Israel. I plead with them to stop going to the temples of Baal. But the idols bring them bountiful harvests and fat children, they say.

You might have seen me haranguing passersby in the market or outside taverns. I'm the one everyone pretends not to see or hear. Pigeons flap around my head, dogs bark, strangers spit on me. Some think I'm a madman. But obeying God is an important thing to do with your life.

My love story starts here: One day I found that I had strong feelings for a woman I had met in the marketplace. Her name was Gomer. When she walked next to me, jewelry chimed happily from her ankles, wrists, and waist. She made a celebration wherever she went. She had a hundred friends and a disappointing reputation. You could say this was an attraction without a future.

No one was more surprised than me when God told me to take her as my wife. "But she is the daughter of Diblaim, a Baal worshiper!" I protested. "What will others think?"

But God didn't change his word to me, so I obeyed. A few weeks later, Gomer and I were married, and I brought her home.

When I took her in my arms, I gave her my heart and my hopes. I was very happy. In the morning, she put away her jewelry and put on the garments of a housewife. Her presence in my life seemed like the tinkling of many bells.

"I would make her happy by the very brightness of my love, I thought."

To a woman used to the color and chatter of city life, my little house just outside the walls of Samaria was quite a shock. Bare whitewashed rooms, bare cupboards, a few scrolls, long silences. The solitude of vineyards sweeping away from our windows. Yes, and a husband who went out every morning to be a spectacle for God. A prophet is a hard husband for a woman with expectations.

She expected at least to help name our children. But when our first son was born, God told me to name him God Scatters. Announce it on the streets, He said. The name was a warning that God would severely punish Israel and the royal family. How could a new mother be happy calling her baby that?

IT WASN'T LONG BEFORE THE LOVELY LIGHT in Gomer's eyes seemed to dim. After a few months, she stopped asking me about news from the streets.

Yet with each step she retreated, my desire for her grew. Perhaps her distances provoked me. Gomer—my Jewish beauty, my own flesh and blood—seemed more than ever a mysterious favor from my God. I would make her happy by the very brightness of my love, I thought. By the wings of my faith, I would carry her to faith.

Out on the streets, God's words seemed to come in torrents:

> Hear the word of the Lord, you Israelites,
> because the Lord has a charge to bring against you who live in the land!
> "There is no faithfulness, no love, no acknowledgement of God in the land.
> There is only cursing, lying and murder, stealing and adultery!
> You stumble day and night,
> and your prophets stumble with you."

Of course, messages like these didn't win bigger audiences.

My Gomer was pregnant again, and this time she gave birth to a sweet little girl. But while Gomer and I were sitting on the bed musing about a name, the Lord said something into my spirit that made me flinch. "Call her Not Loved," he said. "I will no longer show love to my people or forgive them." When I reluctantly told my wife what God had said, she shook her head in stunned disbelief. Her face went pale with rage.

"Who is this savage God you serve?!" she nearly shrieked. "What about me? What about our children? Don't we matter at all?"

A veil of anger settled over my wife after that. She paced the room nursing our baby, shooing God Scatters out of doors, gazing for hours out over the vineyards. She refused to pray with me.

She hardly breathed in my presence. As soon as she was able, she started going out often to visit in the city—with whom, she never said.

What is a man to do when his love is despised? When his own wife tells him with every hollow silence and flinty stare that she dreads his touch and hates her life? A man who can't make the woman he loves happy is no man at all.

Every day I still went to the streets to preach. One morning, after I had finished speaking from the steps of Baal's temple, a beer-breathed stranger leaned close and knifed me in the stomach with his words: "You ever wonder why no one listens to you, preacher? I'll tell you! Your wife, *O man of God . . .* is a common whore." He turned to wave toward the men in the streets. "Just ask around." And then he was gone.

At first I wanted to run after him and choke an apology out of him. These pagans could spit on me, but not on my Gomer! But after the rage passed, I felt only pain. The rest of the day, my words to the crowds came out all cut and bleeding. I crept home hardly alive to my white house.

Gomer returned by dark. I said nothing, but how could my wife not notice my agony? Then the reason came clear. She didn't notice because she didn't care. Her every thought was for another.

And, I soon found out, for his child. She was pregnant again. And why should I think it was my child she carried? Were even our first two mine?

When the third child, a son, was born, God told me his name. It seemed horrible and true: "Call him Not My People," God said. "The people of Samaria are not my people, and I am not their God."

This time I sat beside Gomer in tears. "No more awful lies," I said. We must say what we both knew. This new baby boy, I told her— I knew he wasn't mine, and God knew it, too.

From the bride God gave me, I received only defiant stares. In the morning, Gomer took the baby and our other children, and left.

"Love is not love which alters when it alteration finds."

WILLIAM SHAKESPEARE

Something like calm returned to my whitewashed house above the vineyards. At least now I didn't come home at the end of the day to an enemy, to more humiliating deceptions. And she didn't have to come home at all. It was like the brooding calm between a death and the burial. But when the burial came, it was not, as I expected, the burial of our love, or even of our marriage.

Let me try to explain.

Gomer went her way, finally free. Over the months, I kept track of her whereabouts. She lived with the father of Not My People for a while. Then I heard she had taken another lover. After that, she dropped out of sight.

At least on the streets, more people listened now. And God's words to them lashed like a desert sandstorm—first one way, then another; now with a lion's roar, now with a dove's cooing. I spoke every word. When God raged, I raged. When he begged, I begged. When he wept, I sobbed in front of his people like a lost boy.

Months passed. Word finally reached me that Gomer had sold herself into a brothel. To me it seemed like the end. I pleaded with God for release. By any measure, the time for a divorce had come.

It was a day like any other in the capital when God answered me. The air was thick with the shouts of traders, the smoke of sacrifices, the conspiracies that brewed on every corner. But this time when he spoke to me about Gomer, I thought that God himself had betrayed me.

"Go, show your love to your wife again," he said, "even though she is loved by others and is an adulteress. Love her as I love my people Israel, though they love other gods."

I stumbled home. With every step, with every tear, a new and terrible light broke through. Two love stories—mine and

Love IN BIBLE TIMES

The Picture of Love

The amazing story of Hosea and Gomer's is a picture of an even greater love story—the one between God and His people.

God used Gomer's adultery to point out Israel's unfaithful-ness—and to reveal His own broken heart. "What can I do with you, Ephraim? What can I do with you, Judah? Your love is like the morning mist, like the early dew that disappears" (Hosea 6:4).

Throughout the Bible, the marriage relationship is used as a picture of God's relationship with us. The prophet Isaiah told Israel, "As a bridegroom rejoices over his bride, so will your God rejoice over you" (Isaiah 62:5). Many consider the passionate Song of Songs to be a celebra-tion of God's love affair with His people.

The marriage metaphor appears again in the New Testa-ment—but always in a positive light. Christ compared the king-dom of heaven to a wedding feast. And when Paul wrote to the Ephesians about the union of husband and wife, he said, "This is a profound mystery— but I am [also] talking about Christ and the church" (Ephesians 5:32).

Fittingly, the Bible ends with more images of our marriage to Christ: "Blessed are those who are invited to the wedding supper of the Lamb!" (Revelation 19:9).

my Lord's—had somehow become one story. Two hearts had been broken in the same place.

And now, unaccountably, my God's voice was only tenderness. "I will give her back her vineyards," he whispered in my ear, "and I will make her Valley of Trouble a door of hope."

But how do you show love to a prostitute?

I walked through dusty, broken streets to the brothel, trembling all the way. Inside the door, the brothel keeper looked at me in surprise and disgust. "So, man of God, did you bring money for a girl today?"

"Yes," I replied. "And more. I'm here to buy back Gomer, my wife. I am prepared to pay the full slave price for her."

That is how Gomer and the children came home.

"All I ask is that you be faithful to me," I told her. She was a worn, sad ghost of her former self. She did not wear her jewelry, or put on the garments of marriage. Yet with the gift of her presence, I began to see what Gomer could not see—hope shining over us like an anointing of olive oil. Sometimes I could feel it trickle down our foreheads.

I cared for her morning and evening, and didn't ask her to sleep with me.

OUT ON THE STREETS, word of our story had spread. Crowds gathered. And when I opened my mouth God's voice strummed like a hundred harps above their upturned faces:

> Come, let us return to the Lord
> He has torn us to pieces but he will heal us;
> he has injured us but he will bind up our wounds.
> The Lord says, "I will heal your waywardness and love you freely,
> for my anger has turned away from you.
> I will be like the dew to Israel; you will blossom like a vine."

One evening at home, in the season when the vineyards put on their palest green veil of new leaves, God told me the ending of my love story. I turned to my wife.

"Gomer, my God has spoken to me. He is giving us new names for our children. Our baby boy will no longer be called Not My People, but he will be called My People. And our sweet girl— her name is no longer Not Loved. Her new name is My Loved One."

And I saw a flame like happiness flicker up in my wife's beautiful eyes. ⚘

"With the gift of her presence, I began to see what Gomer could not see—hope..."

MEDITATION
for Married Lovers

Forgiveness, The Way Back

ALL WE KNOW ABOUT Hosea's wife, Gomer, is the worst there is to know: she was a prostitute, unfaithful, a woman who betrayed her husband repeatedly.

But who was Gomer, really? She is given no voice in the biblical account of this story. We don't know what she thought or felt, or what she looked like. We don't even know if she was grateful to be redeemed by her husband.

We do know this much: Faithlessness and betrayal take place on many levels. Jesus said that to look on another with lust is adultery. We could each be guilty, given the right circumstances, of Gomer's sins.

What would have happened if Hosea hadn't reached out to to his rebellious wife first? Would the marriage ever have been put back together? Even if she had wanted to come back, her feelings of guilt, failure, and estrangement from Hosea would probably have kept her away.

And how many of us would not only take back, but pursue, a straying husband or wife who wasn't even sorry?

Hosea's forgiveness of Gomer illustrates God's heart toward Israel—and toward us. He doesn't stop loving us and pursuing us while he waits for us to come to our senses. *"God's kindness leads you toward repentance"* (Romans 2:4).

Our human nature makes it so easy for us to take offense, so hard to extend forgiveness. Yet by the amazing life of Christ, we have everything we need—hope, courage, humility, and understanding—to start over after deep hurts.

Like Gomer, we're capable of terrible sins against our marriage. But by God's grace, we are also like Hosea, candidates for a love that reaches further.

"*He doesn't stop loving us and pursuing us while he waits for us to come to our senses.*"

91

XERXES&ESTHER
Love Is a Shared Kingdom

Sixty queens there may be,

and eighty concubines,

and virgins beyond number;

But my dove, my perfect one, is unique,

the only daughter of her mother,

the favorite of the one who bore her.

The maidens saw her and called her blessed;

the queens and concubines praised her.

Song of Songs 6:8,9

"Sixty queens
there may be,
but my love,

my perfect one,
is unique."

The Marriage:
Esther became King Xerxes' queen by winning an empire-wide beauty contest.

Children:
None mentioned.

Most Memorable Scene:
Xerxes extends his scepter to Esther, thus sparing her life.

Greatest Obstacle:
An unfolding conspiracy to destroy Esther and her people.

Compatibility:
She was a practicing Jew; he was a Persian who practiced the Zoroastrian religion.

Name:
Xerxes (Persian), or Ahasuerus (Greek), "mighty man."

Age:
Unknown.

Appearance:
Portrayed in art of the time as being powerfully built, bearded.

Personality:
Impulsive, short-sighted, but reasonable, fair, and generous.

Family Background:
Father was King Darius Hystaspes of Persia.

Place in History:
Ruler of the vast Persian empire, 485-464 B.C.

"Whatever you I will give

ABOUT HER

Name:
Esther, "a star" (Persian),
or Hadassah, "myrtle" (Hebrew).

Age:
Probably about 15.

Appearance:
Extraordinarily beautiful.

Personality:
Loyal, prudent, confident,
of regal bearing.

Family Background:
Parents deceased;
Esther was adopted and
raised by an older cousin, Mordecai.

Place in History:
The Jewish queen of Persia
who saved God's people
from annihilation.

*request, dear Esther,
even up to half my kingdom—
it to you."*

Love Is a Shared Kingdom

THE BOOK OF ESTHER

When he saw

Queen Esther

ESTHER 5:2

standing in the

court, he was

pleased with her

and held out

to her the gold

scepter that

was in his hand.

EVERYONE IN THE PROVINCE KNEW ABOUT THE ROYAL search for Persia's most beautiful young virgins. And they knew that the girl King Xerxes chose would become the new queen. But somehow Esther never imagined, never dreamed, that the king's officers might someday appear at her door.

When they did, she stood speechless while they explained that they had heard about her beauty, and had come to claim her for King Xerxes' harem. Her older cousin, Mordecai, who had lovingly raised Esther since both of her parents had died, helped her to prepare a few items.

Esther could see by Mordecai's face that he was alarmed, surprised. Mordecai knew as well as Esther that Xerxes held absolute sway over the greatest empire on earth. He owned every life in his kingdom, every property, every orphan girl.

Mordecai repeatedly told Esther, as much for his own sake as for hers, "It will be all right, my dear Esther. They will be kind to you."

For the next year, Esther was pampered with the finest oils, perfumes, baths, cosmetics, and special foods. Along with the other young beauties swirling about the harem, Esther was carefully schooled in the nuances of royal life. And with them, she awaited the king's summons.

Yet Esther alone kept a dangerous secret. On Mordecai's instructions, she didn't reveal to anyone that she was a Jew.

Even in a harem of such splendor, Esther's remarkable beauty and spirit set her apart. She completely won over the harem master, Hegai. Soon he was lavishing privileges on her, giving her the best of everything, and assigning seven maids to attend her. "I am wise to give special care to the one who may someday be my queen!" he told her.

Esther wasn't sure what to hope for. Hadn't Xerxes banished his first queen, the lovely Vashti? If ever the king *did* choose Esther, what would he do when he discovered that he had married a Jew? And yet, to not be chosen would mean a life of pampered luxury in the king's harem. Some of the girls thought this a marvelous life. But Esther still sighed over her girlish dream of marrying a good Jewish boy.

One by one the girls around Esther were taken to the king. Finally it was Esther's turn. She went to the palace dressed exactly as Hegai advised. Her pulse raced as the harem master escorted her down colonnaded hallways, past armed guards, and into the king's personal chamber.

The next morning, King Xerxes announced that he had found his queen.

A few days later at a great banquet in her honor, he set a crown on young Esther's head, and introduced her as queen in Vashti's place. Esther had already sensed that Xerxes would treat her honorably. But now she saw something else in his eyes that surprised her—perhaps he even loved her. For his part, to show his empire how happy he was, Xerxes proclaimed a national holiday with royal favors for all.

"Now she saw something else in his eyes—perhaps he even loved her."

Being married to Xerxes suited Esther more than she had ever dreamed. But palace life in Susa, the capital of the Persian empire, was anything but tranquil. Xerxes' armies waged war continually from Greece in the west to India in the east. In the palace itself, petty rebellions brewed. Esther was shocked when Mordecai himself uncovered one plot to assassinate King Xerxes. When he sent word of the plot to Xerxes through Esther, the conspirators were hanged.

THEN ONE DAY ESTHER'S MAIDS TOLD HER that Mordecai was mourning publicly at the palace gate. He wore sackcloth and ashes they said, and wailed loudly about impending doom. Esther hurriedly sent a servant to find out what was wrong. He returned to the queen's quarters with a copy of a decree written by Haman, the king's chief counselor.

This decree set a date for the murder of all Jews—young and old, women and children included. Anyone who joined in the slaughter was invited afterwards to plunder Jewish property and belongings. And Xerxes had signed the decree himself! "How did such a calamity come about?" Esther cried.

"Love me not for comely grace, for my pleasing eye or face, nor for any outward part..."
ANONYMOUS

97

It all began, the servant confided, when Mordecai refused to kneel before Haman when he passed by. Haman was a proud, power-hungry official who hated Jews, and Mordecai's stubbornness enraged him.

Mordecai had also sent an urgent personal request. Esther must go into Xerxes' presence and beg for mercy for her people.

But Esther knew that this would be impossible. She sent a hastily written explanation back to Mordecai:

"Any man or woman who enters the king's presence without being summoned will be put to death. The only exception to this is if the king holds out the gold scepter—then the person's life is spared. And I don't know if I still please the king; he hasn't asked for me to come to his chambers for 30 days."

Esther's reasons did not sway Mordecai. He fired back an impassioned reply.

"Do not think that because you are in the king's house you alone of all the Jews will escape," he wrote. *"If you remain silent now, deliverance for the Jews will arise from another place, but you and your family will die. But consider, you may have been brought to your royal position for just such a time as this!"*

For such a time as this? A window seemed to open in Esther's spirit. For the first time, she sensed that a larger plan might be at work in her life. Perhaps a Jewish orphan had been God's choice all along to be Queen of Persia.

This time, she sent a different message to the Jew at the gate:

"Ask all our people in the city to pray and fast for three days and nights. I and my maids will do the same. Afterwards, I will go to the king, even though it is against the law. If I perish, I perish."

Inside the queen's chambers, Esther fasted and prayed with her maids. Where once they had prepared the lovely Esther with every indulgence for her king, now they prepared her with humility and hunger. Their prayers in the night seemed more like ointments for a burial than for a marriage bed.

Esther carefully considered her course. Was the king's affection for her deep enough to compel him to reach for the scepter? Would he forgive her deception about being a Jew? She knew that

> ## "But consider, you may have been brought to your royal position *for just such a time as this!*"

The morning after the fast was over, Esther put on her royal robes, entered the inner court of the palace, and stood at the door to King Xerxes' throne room. Her heart caught when Xerxes looked up and noticed her standing there. She saw the look in his eyes—gladness and love—and watched with relief as he stretched the gold scepter in her direction.

AS SHE APPROACHED THE THRONE, the array of startled court advisers parted before her.

"What is it, Queen Esther?" asked Xerxes. "Whatever your request is—even up to half my kingdom—I will give it to you."

A small ripple of exclamation sounded among those present. Esther looked directly into the king's kind eyes, and she smiled and bowed. "If it please my lord," replied Esther, "come today to a banquet I have prepared for you. And let chief counselor Haman come with you."

"Absolutely!" exclaimed her husband. "Notify Haman at once!" he ordered an aide. "We will do what you ask, my queen."

That day at Esther's private, lavish feast, while the king and Haman were relaxing over wine, the king again asked Esther to tell him her request. "Please, do tell me, my dear queen. Even up to half of my kingdom, whatever you want will be yours."

Again, Esther surprised him. "If you regard me with favor, and if it would please my king to grant my petition, then please come again tomorrow to a banquet I will prepare for you and Haman. At that time, I will reveal to you my request."

The next day, again over goblets of wine, the king asked his wife to tell him her request and offered half his kingdom.

she must sway the king's heart without insulting his pride. Vashti had questioned his authority to her doom.

Love IN BIBLE TIMES

The Romance of Food

"He has taken me to the banquet hall, and his banner over me is love."
Song of Songs 2:4

Throughout Bible times, culinary delights and romance often shared the same table, as when Xerxes gave a banquet for his new bride. Such a feast would have been an opulent affair, with exotic foods and "goblets of gold, each one different than the other."

The swooning lovers in Song of Songs often linked food and love: "Strengthen me with raisins, refresh me with apples, for I am faint with love" (Song of Songs 2:5). Sometimes a gift of food indicated affection or honor. Boaz filled Ruth's apron with grain. Elkanah provided his sad Hannah with an extra portion of meat.

Fruit, in particular, has long been associated with the power to seduce. Adam and Eve fell into sin through eating a forbidden fruit. Jews were fond of the scarlet pomegranate, and believed that, with its fleshy texture and abundance of seeds, it could aid fertility.

But the romance of food goes beyond sensual passions. Both food and love satisfy strong human hungers—one of the stomach, and one of the heart. To this day, whenever we express our affections with chocolates or a dinner by candlelight, we repeat an ancient invitation, "Come, my darling, taste and see that love is good!"

"If I have found favor with you, O king, and if it pleases your majesty, spare my life...and spare the lives of my people."

The time had come for Esther to tell the king her secret. "If I have found favor with you, O King," she began, "and if it pleases Your Majesty, spare my life. This is my request. And spare the lives of my people."

The king and Haman both looked stunned. Esther continued, "My people and I have been sold for slaughter. If we had merely been sold as slaves, I would not be troubling my king with this request."

"But who is the enemy who would dare to do such a thing?" King Xerxes nearly shouted.

"My lord," Esther replied, "the enemy is this man, Haman."

Haman had turned deathly white. Xerxes, speechless with rage and astonishment, stormed from the room.

In a desperate move, Haman threw himself across Esther's couch and groveled for mercy. When the king strode back into the room moments later, he saw Haman clinging to his wife.

"Will this man even molest the queen in my own house?" he exclaimed. Esther watched as the king's guards dragged the doomed Haman away. Then one of them told the king that Haman had built a 75 foot gallows on which he'd planned to hang Mordecai—"the man who spoke up to save the king's life from an assassination plot," he said.

"Hang Haman on his own gallows!" the king bellowed.

LATER THAT SAME DAY, ESTHER SPOKE AGAIN WITH KING XERXES, explaining to him that her people, the Jews, were not disloyal to the king, only bound by their faith to the one God of Israel. Mordecai, Xerxes' loyal servant, was her cousin and adoptive father, she said. Would the king be willing to issue another edict overruling Haman's decree?

"Of course, my beloved Esther," he answered. "Write another decree in the king's name as seems best to you. And I will seal it with my signet ring."

By then it was evening, and they were alone in his chambers. Xerxes' tone had softened. His kind glances indicated to Esther that she would not be leaving before morning. And she was glad.

The next day, Xerxes' fastest horsemen raced throughout Persia informing everyone that the Jews' lives had been spared. Only later would God's grateful people learn that their salvation had come from a young queen who had dared to both honor and sway the heart of her king.

The Power of Two

AT FIRST GLANCE, the story of Esther can offend our modern sensibilities. A king who deposes his queen when she refuses to be ogled by her husband's friends at a party? Who collects for himself a harem of beautiful virgins as if they exist only for his pleasure?

Yet the kind of power Xerxes wielded was standard for a monarchy at the time. A king was viewed as a kind of god. What was *not* usual was Xerxes' love for his new bride—despite her social status as an orphaned peasant. Xerxes appears to have admired Esther so greatly that what could have been an ancient war of the sexes gave way to a relationship of mutual respect, admiration, and support.

The king was so smitten with his new queen that he offered her half his kingdom—three times. More than just a figure of speech, the king was saying, "Let's be partners, my love. I'm willing to share my power with you!"

Such words were priceless to Esther—not because she wanted the kingdom, or even to usurp the king's position. She hoped to wield influence with Xerxes so that she could avert a tragedy and alert him to Haman's abuse of royal trust and authority.

For centuries, issues of male dominance and female manipulation have brought hurt and disharmony into marriages. In reality, as husbands and wives we hold scepters of influence or authority in our hands every day.

Loving is never safe. When we give love, we give away power to hurt or heal. We give away what's precious to us, up to half the kingdom—and maybe more.

And yet, when both partners wield their powers wisely and humbly—"submitting one to another" (Ephesians 5:21)—we become stronger, not weaker. For greater is the power of two in the kingdom of marriage.

"Loving is never safe. When we give love, we give away power."

JOSEPH&MARY
Love Is God with Us

Like a lily among thorns

is my darling among the maidens...

Like an apple tree among the trees of the forest

is my lover among the young men.

I delight to sit in his shade,

and his fruit is sweet to my taste.

He has taken me to the banquet hall,

and his banner over me is love.

Song of Songs 2:3,4

"His banner over me is love."

MARY & JOSEPH

The Marriage:
An angel directed Joseph to marry his pregnant fiancée.

Children:
Five sons, including Jesus, plus daughters.

Most Memorable Scene:
When the angel Gabriel comes to Mary to announce her special mission.

Greatest Obstacle:
Concern over public humiliation when it was learned that Mary had become pregnant out of wedlock.

Compatibility:
Very high; a shared and deeply felt devotion to God.

Elizabeth consoled

He may

ABOUT HIM

Name:
Joseph, "increaser."

Age:
Unknown, probably around 25.

Appearance:
Unknown.

Personality:
Faithful, reliable, described as "righteous."

Family Background:
Son of Jacob, a descendant of David; his hometown was Bethlehem.

Place in History:
The loyal husband of Mary, the mother of Jesus.

ABOUT HER

Name:
Mary, "strong."

Age:
Unknown, probably about 15.

Appearance:
Unknown.

Personality:
Gracious, full of faith, forthright, willing, wise.

Family Background:
From Nazareth in Galilee; like her husband, she was from the tribe of Judah.

Place in History:
The virgin who became the mother of Jesus, Son of God.

her— "Joseph is a good and righteous man. even believe you!"

Love Is God with Us
LUKE 1,2; MATTHEW 1

Joseph, son of

David, do not

be afraid to take

Mary home

as your wife,

because what

MATTHEW 1:20

is conceived

in her is from

the Holy Spirit.

MARY ROLLED OVER IN HER BED for the hundredth time. How was she ever supposed to go to sleep again?

The wedding feast was still a long way off. But she had felt restless ever since that night three weeks ago when Joseph and his father had come to ask for her hand in marriage. She could still hear her dear father's quavering voice when he turned to Joseph and said, "You have obtained for yourself a wife beyond price."

Afterward, Joseph's eyes had met her own briefly—she could still remember their exact shade of light brown—as if to inquire if she were happy with the arrangement.

How had she answered his look? She couldn't remember. She only hoped her mouth hadn't been hanging open foolishly, or that her eyes hadn't given away her frightened but utter happiness.

At first, Mary hadn't known what to think of Joseph. He was handsome in a warm, gentle way. But he was also quiet, and so serious! Yet, the last time she'd seen him, something about the corners of his mouth had let her know that he could laugh as easily as a brook babbles.

And, in the end, the steady way Joseph carried himself had spoken deeply to her heart.

Tonight, as she lay awake in her bed, she wondered again what kind of husband Joseph would be. Would he like to talk, or to walk beneath the stars? Would he be gentle with her? Would he notice her meals, and the careful way she would make a lovely home for them? She had observed many husbands who never seemed to notice much. . . .

She sighed, and swung her legs out from under the covers. She was about to go for a drink of water when suddenly something made her start and turn. She froze with fear. There, at the foot of her bed, stood a brilliant, glowing being. An angel!

She was so filled with terror that she was unable to move, or even to think. But the angel's voice reassured her. "Greetings, you who are highly favored! The Lord is with you."

Mary's mind raced. She had heard of angels visiting women in the past. But what kind of visit was this? And what could he mean by "highly favored"?

Then the angel spoke again. *"Do not be afraid, Mary, you have found favor with God. You will be with child and give birth to a son, and you are to give him the name Jesus"* (Luke 1:30,31). The angel spoke slowly, carefully. But Mary's head whirled with confusion. Was the angel talking of Joseph? But they were only just betrothed, and still a long way off from babies.

"Was the angel talking of Joseph? But they were only just betrothed, and still a long way off from babies."

"He will be great," the angel went on, *"and will be called the Son of the Most High. The Lord God will give him the throne of his father David, and he will reign over the house of Jacob forever; his kingdom will never end"* (Luke 1:32,33).

Mary hesitated. "How will this happen," she finally asked, "since I am a virgin?"

How strange to be discussing such a thing with an angel!

But the heavenly being seemed to expect her question. *"The Holy Spirit will come upon you,"* he answered. *"And the power of the Most High will overshadow you. So the holy one to be born will be called the Son of God. Even Elizabeth your relative is going to have a child in her old age, and she who was said to be barren is in her sixth month. For nothing is impossible with God"* (Luke 1:35-37).

Mary knew that what the angel had spoken was true. Her heart pounded. She wanted to do whatever God asked of her. How she had always loved the Lord! Even as a child—the hymns, the prayers, the incense at the temple . . . If God were going to give her a special task, she would not refuse it!

"I am the Lord's servant," she answered evenly. *"May it be to me as you have said"* (Luke 1:38).

AFTER THE ANGEL LEFT, Mary sat unmoving for many minutes, staring at the spot where the angel had been. She rubbed her eyes repeatedly and tried to recall every word he had spoken. She was to bear the Son of God! She! The idea was so wondrous and inconceivable that it was quite some time before another thought hit her. *Joseph! What about Joseph? Why hadn't she asked the angel more?*

The next morning, Mary decided to go see her older cousin Elizabeth. It was so hard to believe. Elizabeth pregnant? At her age? And perhaps for that very reason, she would be a welcoming soul for Mary to share her own news with.

"The virtue which does her adorn, by honor guarded, not by scorn."

KATHERINE PHILLIPS

Mary hurried to Elizabeth's house in the hill country of Judea. As soon as her cousin Elizabeth saw her, she exclaimed, *"Blessed are you among women, and blessed is the child you will bear! But why am I so favored, that the mother of my Lord should come to me?"* (Luke 1:42,43).

Mary was elated. Elizabeth was not only obviously pregnant herself, but she somehow knew what Mary suspected—Mary was *already* pregnant with God's own baby!

MARY SPENT THREE JOYOUS MONTHS with Elizabeth. They laughed aloud every day to think of what miracles God was performing. And he had chosen them—a virgin and a woman past childbearing age—to bear sons that would deliver the world from their sin!

Even so, now and then, a shadow crossed Mary's face. One day, while they were quietly preparing bread for the evening meal, Elizabeth gently asked, "Are you worrying about Joseph again?"

"What will I say to him?" Mary's tone was pleading. "How does one explain to a man to whom one is betrothed that one is going to have a baby, and not by him, or by any man, but by God? If I had not seen an angel, I wouldn't believe such a story!"

"You are worrying yourself too much," Elizabeth consoled her. "Joseph is a good and righteous man. He may even believe you," she added somewhat doubtfully. "But are you willing, my dear, if necessary. . . to be scorned and rejected for the cause of the Lord's anointed?"

"Oh!" Mary cried. "But of course! It's not that. It's just that . . . to have Joseph think such things to be true of me. I dreamed that I might come to love Joseph and he might love me. Now, I can't imagine . . . "

Finally, Mary knew it was time for her to return home and face whatever waited for her there. Soon, it would be apparent to all that she was expecting a baby. Soon, people would look at her and stare.

On the way home, she felt terribly ill at ease, and it seemed as if, for once, the donkey she rode on was moving *faster* than necessary. When she finally arrived home, however, it was not her mother who came out to greet her, but Joseph.

His face looked eager and his eyes were bright. "Mary!" he cried. "My Mary!"

He helped her to dismount and brought water for her feet. "You cannot wait on me!" Mary objected. "Where is my mother?"

"She has made a trip to the market. And I have been waiting here for you, my sweet Mary. I have spoken at some length with your parents already. And I wanted to see you as soon as possible to tell you the good news!"

Mary wanted to interrupt, to stop him, to stop his kindnesses, to send him away perhaps, until she could compose herself, until she had a plan that—

"I know that you are with child, Mary!" Joseph declared.

Mary gasped. "You . . . you know?"

"And I know that the baby you bear is God's!" cried Joseph. "At first, when I heard the rumor that you were pregnant, I was in bitter anguish. I did not want to divorce you, my Mary. But I was going to . . . "

Mary had never before heard Joseph say so much at once.

"And then an angel came to me in a dream," he continued, "and told me to marry you! The angel said that this child was to be named Jesus, and that he would save the people from their sins! He is to be Emmanuel, Mary! 'God with us!'" . . .

AND SO MARY AND JOSEPH WERE QUICKLY MARRIED, and the wedding feast was attended by many, both because of and in spite of the rumor that Mary was already with child. But when the two were led to the bridal chamber and left to consummate their marriage, Joseph only held Mary close all night. "The angel told me I am not to lie with you until you have the baby," he said.

Love IN BIBLE TIMES

Love in the Houses of History

Open the book of Matthew to read about Mary and Joseph, and you come first to the genealogy of Jesus. Though it's tempting to skip over these long lists of "begots," they remind us that romance, love, and marriage are not an end unto themselves, but a critical part of God's bigger plan.

Such genealogies—usually compiled to celebrate first-born sons—were of utmost importance to the Jews. Tracing one's descent was necessary to claim a family inheritance. And since the Messiah was to come through David's house, proof of Davidic ancestry was carefully preserved.

Naturally, every women in David's line hoped to give birth to the promised child.

One way to view the Bible is as a collection of four family sagas, where each epic story leads forward to the dramatic event of Christ's birth, and the extension of God's family to include all believers.

The Family of Adam—The beginnings of the human race (Adam and Eve)

The Family of Abraham—The origins of the 12 tribes of Israel (Abraham and Sarah)

The Family of David—The dynasty of kings that ruled the nation for almost 500 years (David and Bathsheba)

The Family of Jesus—Adopted into the house of God by the redeeming work of Jesus Christ (Joseph and Mary)

At that moment, Mary knew that she would indeed love Joseph, and perhaps she already did! For what kind of man but the most wonderful kind would have such faith? And would agree to wait for his wife to bear a baby before consummating his marriage?

In the months that followed, Joseph never seemed to waver, even as Mary's belly grew. And even as, night after night, Mary felt Joseph hold back his own longings for her.

Then, just when her pregnancy was feeling interminably long—*why wouldn't a baby that God made come faster?*—more hard news arrived. She and Joseph would have to travel to Bethlehem, Joseph's home town, to register for a census ordered by Caesar Augustus. Tomorrow they would begin the journey—and with Mary's tummy as large as a water jug.

> *"What kind of man but the most wonderful kind would have such faith?"*

All day, Mary worked hard packing for the trip, preparing foods, folding up clothing. By the time darkness fell, her back ached, and her feet had swollen to a size much closer to Joseph's than her own.

For his part, Joseph also looked tired and worn. Older than his years. But still he wanted to walk with Mary under the stars of Nazareth one last time before their journey. As they strolled to the edge of the village, he put an arm around Mary and held her close. After some time, he asked her in a quiet voice, "Are you ready, my love?"

She knew that he was asking her about more than the trip. Was she ready?

She turned and sought Joseph's eyes in the moonlight. She couldn't make out their soft shade of brown, but she could see it vividly in her imagination. "I wish he were going to have your eyes," she said wistfully.

Joseph stopped walking and turned to face her before he whispered, "And perhaps he will, my Mary. Remember the angel's words? 'With God, nothing is impossible.'"

Mary smiled broadly then, and she also began to feel a little sleepy. Yes, tomorrow morning they would begin a journey. Who knew exactly where it would lead? But she was sure of this: God had chosen Joseph to be this baby's father—just as surely as he had chosen her to be the mother!

And then husband and wife walked home under a brilliant, starlit sky, their thoughts filled with new hope for the One to come. And their hearts filled with a love that had already arrived.

The Greatest Story

AS WE COME TO THE FINAL LOVE STORY in the Bible, an ordinary carpenter and his young, pregnant bride begin a journey toward Bethlehem—and the unknown. Others making the same dusty trip could never have guessed how God was using Mary and Joseph's relationship in his amazing plan of redemption.

Ever since Adam and Eve, God has been placing his designs in the hands of ordinary couples. And each couple has had to choose whether or not to move forward in faith, answering in their own way the question first put to Eve, "Did God *really* say . . . ?"

"Did God *really* say your descendants would be blessed?" . . . "Did God *really* say to take back your wayward wife?" Just imagine Joseph's thoughts during that first nine months! "Did the angel *really* say. . . ?"

Like others before them, Mary and Joseph were invited to make a leap of faith in God—and in each other.

They answered *yes*. Simply. Beautifully. "Let it be done to me as you have said," declared Mary.

God could have chosen a couple with a proven marriage—or skipped the marriage (and parents) altogether. Instead, the God of the universe made himself vulnerable to two human hearts with only the promise and potential of love ahead—as if to say, "Without a choice to love, I don't really even want this plan."

How blessed we are that God doesn't ask us to take a leap of love alone. He takes one with us. In so many wonderful ways he pursues our hearts! He is our Creator who knows us completely. He is our Matchmaker who goes ahead of us. He is our Beloved who will pay any price for us. He is our Kinsman who redeems us, and our Bridegroom who prepares a home for us.

In fact, God's own love for us turns out to be the greatest love story he ever told. "For God so loved the world, that he gave his one and only Son, that whoever believes in him shall not perish, but have eternal life" (John 3:16).

"*God's own love for us turns out to be the greatest love story ever told.*"

111